Saints in Action

Saints in Action

DUMAS MALONE

Essay Index Reprint Series

BOOKS FOR LIBRARIES PRESS
FREEPORT, NEW YORK

First Published 1939
Reprinted 1971

INTERNATIONAL STANDARD BOOK NUMBER:
0-8369-2062-7

LIBRARY OF CONGRESS CATALOG CARD NUMBER:
70-142664

PRINTED IN THE UNITED STATES OF AMERICA

TO THE MEMORY OF
MY FATHER

TABLE OF CONTENTS

FOREWORD

THIS book comprises lectures that were delivered to popular audiences at Drew University in March, 1939, and that are reproduced here in practically their original form. They represent the attempt of a layman, who is not a specialist in religious history or biography, to draw illustrations of saintliness from the rich record of American achievement as a whole and to apply to the deeds of certain religious men and women the tests of honest but finite personal judgment.

For convenience I have treated these historic figures in groups rather than as isolated individuals and I have freely availed myself not only of individual biographies but also of the collective judgments that are embodied in the *Dictionary of American Biography*, with which I was so intimately associated. In the chapters on the clergy and women saints the achievements of groups are surveyed and statistics are cited, but nowhere is there any pretense of comprehensiveness. I hope, therefore, that I shall not be taxed with glaring omissions or with errors of selection.

For my personal judgments the sponsors of the lectures are not to blame. I am deeply grate-

ful to them for having given me the opportunity
to live again in spirit with a goodly number of
great Americans of the past, along with a few
others whom I do not esteem so highly.

DUMAS MALONE.

Cambridge, Massachusetts
May 10, 1939

I

THE VARIETIES OF SAINTLINESS IN AMERICA

ACCORDING to William James, the best collective name for the ripe fruits of religion in a character is saintliness. "The saintly character," he says, "is the character for which spiritual emotions are the habitual center of the personal energy; and there is a certain composite photograph of universal saintliness, the same in all religions, of which the features can easily be traced."[1] Saints are to be found in no single sect but in all sects: among Protestants and Catholics, among Christians, Mohammedans, and Jews, even among men who recognize no corporate church and would be described by some as unbelievers. This thought came to the mind of a young American woman traveling in Europe more than half a century ago. Jane Addams, meditating in a German cathedral before she sought to establish a "cathedral of humanity" in Chicago, saw in the carvings on the choir stalls not only Hebrew prophets, but also Greek philosophers and even builders of pagan temples. Late in the night she recorded in her

[1] *The Varieties of Religious Experience* (1914), p. 271.

notebook that "the saints but embodied fine action."[2]

We may readily agree that they shall be known by their fruits and their spirit, not by their doctrines or church connections, but, despite what William James said about the ease of tracing the features of universal saintliness, it seems doubtful that saints have been, are, or ever will be universally recognized. The opinions of contemporaries about the character and spirit of any individual vary enormously, and not even posterity gives a unanimous verdict. If we may believe certain newspaper stories, Adolf Hitler is regarded by some of his compatriots as a god, of a rude Teutonic sort, but to most of the Czechs and all of the Jews he seems a demon. The former president of Czecho-Slovakia, Eduard Beneš, is undoubtedly an heroic and in many respects a saintly figure to most members of his race, but he was described in the summer of 1938 by German Nazis as the incarnation of falsehood. These widespread divergences in contemporary opinion may be attributed in part at least to differences in the information that is available to those who pass judgment, as well as to variations in criteria. Controlled propaganda can make of any man a hero or a devil.

However, even after passions have cooled and

---

[2] *Twenty Years at Hull House* (1910), pp. 82-83.

calm students have appeared as assessors of evidence, difference of opinion often continues. Even now there is doubt in some minds whether John Brown was a hero or a madman. Posterity judges men considerably if not chiefly in terms of their objectives. The hero is a man who has fought impressively for a cause of which we approve. If we do not like his cause, we may term him a fanatic or even a villain. It is easy to explain differences of local opinion about Hitler, about Cardinal Innitzer, about General Franco, even about Pius XI.

The fanatic and the saint may differ in objectives and in intelligence, but they are alike in that they are driven by powerful emotion. It is this, whether it be love or hate, that gives them singleness of mind and invincibility of will. They are less subject than the rest of us to ordinary fears and inhibitions. The essence of saintliness is its spirit, which derives from spiritual emotions and about which our judgment must always be to greater or less degree imperfect.

One hesitates, therefore, to dub anyone a saint, especially if his deeds have been performed outside the recognized religious sphere. However, saintliness, more or less imperfect in form, can be perceived better than it can be described; and about its presence in the character of a particular person there can be a fair consensus of informed opinion. Francis of Assisi and Robert E. Lee, Oliver Cromwell and Jane Addams lived at different times and did very different things. Only one of them has been canonized officially, but in all of them spiritual emotions were strong and central. It would appear that saintliness is of great variety.

Those saints who are most honored in history have been more than negative, so the common opinion that the saint exemplifies the passive virtues alone is not warranted. However, in ages of violence he may be able to do little else. To the militant nationalists of contemporary Europe, glorifying the ways of tribal force, religious charity and forbearance doubtless seem beneath contempt. Men who are attune to another, and in our opinion a higher life, may be able to survive only by practicing quiet patience and endurance in a clamorous world, hoping that flowers may bloom again after the hurricane is spent. In times of violence in the past, monasteries arose as havens and fortresses of the spirit. Even the physical form of some of these retreats exemplified their double and defensive purpose, as notably at Mont Saint Michel. There are places in the world today where the saint faces the alternative of quietism or annihilation. It is already evident that the day of spiritual martyrdom has returned.

In historic America there has been less occasion for monastic retreat from physical violence, and in recent generations at least it has not been necessary for the religious life to assume such unworldly form. It is far from improbable that it has suffered some loss of quality because of a compromising spirit, but certainly that land is fortunate where men can attain a degree of saintliness without peril to their lives. Whatever may be the reasons, or our interpretation of them, our spiritual heroes have not played primarily a contemplative rôle. In our land the religious impulse has expressed itself more characteristically in some form of activity, which has often been in no sense ecclesiastical. Even in the spiritual sphere this vigorous young society of ours has produced, most notably, men of action.

Without defining terms too sharply, we shall draw upon the rich storehouse of American biography for examples of saintliness, and shall attempt to apply to religious men and women the test of achievement and historical significance. If it be true in general, as William James has said, that "the best fruits of religious experience are the best things that history has to show," what may be said of the American harvest? How abundant has it been, and how diverse? It is quite impossible to measure the influence of the religious spirit in this country or any other, but in reverence and honesty we can attempt to measure the achievements of some of our saints and their importance in our history.

Our first task, however, is to survey the diverse American field, though without pretense of comprehensiveness, and to inquire where saints have appeared. If we look for them, we can find them in almost every sphere of activity, even on the field of battle. Of the numerous military examples I shall mention only two, with whose careers almost everybody is familiar; their advocacy of a lost cause has not dimmed their glory in our history.

Though he fought beside American Cavaliers, Stonewall Jackson might have marched in his great boots or ridden on "Little Sorrel" with Cromwell's army. It is doubtful if the military annals of the world will reveal a more profoundly religious warrior. The emotional power which drove him on and which he imparted to his lagging men was re-enforced by solitude and prayer, and, though critics acclaim him a military genius, he undoubtedly thought of himself as a soldier of the Lord.

On the subject of Robert E. Lee both Northern and Southern writers have long been lyrical. Of his greatness as a soldier and a human being there is now no question, but it has remained for his definitive biographer to make clear that in his Christian gentility lay not only his chief strength but also his greatest weakness. In connection with an early and unsuccessful campaign in western Virginia, Douglas Freeman has made a comment which seems destined to become classic: "Of some other commanders in the great American tragedy one might have to ask whether they were drunk or sober on a given day, whether they were indolent or aggressive, whether they lost their heads in the emergency or mastered themselves. Of Lee it became necessary to ask, for two years and more, whether his judgment as a soldier or his consideration as a gentleman dominated his acts."[3] He was no cruel egoist, trampling with iron heel upon those who did not see with him, but "a simple soul, humble, transparent, and believing. Whatever befell the faithful was the will of God, and whatever God willed was best."

It is difficult not to become sentimental in speaking of such a man, and in the South at least he was deified long ago. "We had heard of God," said one Virginia girl, "but here was General Lee." Perhaps the worst comment that can be made on him is that he seems almost too good to be true, and that to a cynical generation his piety

[3] *R. E. Lee* (New York, Scribner's, 1934), Vol. I, p. 553.

may at times seem suffocating.[4] It is certainly no
reflection on the triumphant cause of the Union,
for which so many brave and good men fought
and died, to say that Lee is our supreme Christian
soldier. The temporary objectives for which he
and others strove may seem to later generations
either right or wrong, or a mixture of the two.
On both sides of this and other conflicts there
were saints in armor, divergent in object but kin-
dred in soul.

In the arena of politics the odor of sanctity
generally is faint. Formal church connections,
of course, are a valuable political asset among a
conventionally religious people, but all too often
officeholders and candidates bow the knee to the
god of expediency. Self-abnegation is uncom-
mon except in moments of national peril. It is
rare indeed during periods of great prosperity
and power in the state.

One hesitates, therefore, to select candidates
for canonization from the political roster. Washington and Lincoln have been immortalized in
shaft and enshrined in temple. So much has
been written about them that nothing need be
said here except that, while numerous human
frailties have been discovered in both of them

[4] From my own review of Freeman's *R. E. Lee*, in *American Historical Review*, October, 1935, pp. 167-68, upon which I have drawn
freely.

by industrious investigators, they remain as pre-eminent symbols of high character. To them we have properly attributed patriotism that is in essence spiritual. However, we don't think of Benjamin Franklin as soaring to heaven, like his famous kite. His philosophy was of a superbly mundane sort, his wisdom was great but it was worldly, and he would have chuckled had any-one called him saintly. Jefferson is little short of a political saint in his native region and else-where, and unquestionably his civic faith was magnificent, but the rationalism of the Sage of Monticello was of the mind rather than the heart. Henry Clay, who cast an idolatrous spell over a generation, was in spirit a gamester; and his colossal colleague, Daniel Webster, was more godlike upon the rostrum than in private life.

John Quincy Adams was unquestionably righteous, not to say self-righteous; and during his last years, in connection with the antislavery movement, he manifested high moral fervor. Admirable he was and brave, but if he was a saint he certainly was not lovable; and one sus-pects from the self-conscious entries in his diary that he communed with his own stern soul rather than with an infinitely compassionate God. Oddly enough, John C. Calhoun also appears as a Puritan in politics. In this Scotch-Irishman, who gained so much of his education in Connecti-

cut and whose historic fame is chiefly that of a
political theologian, one may detect considerable
resemblance to John Calvin. Upon the Southern
people he fastened a body of political dogma as
logical and gloomy as Calvinism and from it
they have never quite escaped. His integrity
and intellectual stature are now everywhere
acknowledged, but it is chiefly in South Carolina
that he is likely to be referred to as Saint John.

James G. Blaine was dubbed a plumed knight
by Robert G. Ingersoll, and with diabolical irony
the cartoonist Thomas Nast put the plumes in
his top hat, but no one would now think of re-
placing them with a halo. Another unsuccessful
candidate for the Presidency, though regarded
as a demon in financial circles in the East, was
esteemed by church people throughout the West
and South as a profoundly religious man. The
extraordinary oratory of William Jennings
Bryan might have been employed in the pulpit
as well as the political convention. That he was
a fundamentalist opponent of evolution in the
1920's proves no more than does the allegation
that he was an economic heretic in 1896. More
important in this discussion is the fact that this
Presbyterian elder proclaimed a political crusade
with the warmth and eloquence of a Whitefield.
If not a lay saint, he was unquestionably a lay
evangelist—full-blooded and warm-hearted,

championing the cause of the unfortunate with unrivaled zeal. Opinions differ about his intelligence, but the emotional springs of his power were not unlike those by which religious evangelism has always been watered. The chief whom he served after his own presidential ambitions were surrendered was of colder and harder Calvinistic type, for Bryan, though a Presbyterian, was in spirit an evangelical. The intellectuality of Woodrow Wilson, however, could not entirely mask the religious zeal which made him not only a Covenanter, as he said, but also a domestic reformer and the most conspicuous modern crusader for the cause of international peace. There were hidden fires in the soul of the man who for a brief time was heralded in Europe as a Messiah. These were kindled by his father in home and pulpit and were never suffocated by learning. No one can understand Woodrow Wilson if he ignores the essentially religious nature of the man. That he had some of the mannerisms of a clergyman is a triviality; that he preached from Washington to a world-wide congregation is an important historical fact; that his zeal was warmed by inner fires such as always burn in the hearts of religious devotees is most important of all. Neither he nor his Secretary of State had the self-abnegation of the martyr, and both of them lived amid the worldly compromises of politics, but, more than most of our statesmen, they were attuned to an inner world, as saints have always been.

In the Pantheon of American literature, as of world literature, there are both saints and sinners; but men of letters, more often than office-holders, appear to have been fed by inner springs of spiritual power. One does not perceive saintliness, as we have described it, in the melancholy abnormalities of Edgar Allan Poe. This sad singer of haunting lyrics and teller of grotesque tales never found the serenity and unconquerable resolution which communion with unseen powers has so often brought. That the robust irreverence of Mark Twain was of the frontier rather than the cloister may for our purposes be unimportant, but it is significant that this inveterate traveler revealed by his restlessness that he was not at home with the universe or with himself. Saints carry their heaven with them and are prone to be everywhere content. There may have been a sort of egocentric spirituality in Walt Whitman, but the claims of the poet in gray to unconventional saintliness are marred by strong suspicions that as a man he was a poseur. The religious spirit appears more conspicuously in the gentleness of the decorous Longfellow, even though he had little of the asceticism of the devotee. It appears also in the hymns and crusades of John Greenleaf Whittier; and, to some extent perhaps, more gloomily, in the works of Nathaniel Hawthorne, who grew up in solitude and wrote of sin.

Unquestionably, it is manifest in the Sage of Concord, best beloved and most honored of American men of letters. Emerson might have sat for a portrait in William James's gallery of saints. For his simple wants he had to eke out his small income with his pen and his lecture tours, but he remained master of his soul. To conventional theologians this descendant of a line of clergymen who abandoned the ministry because he regarded the profession as antiquated, may still be suspect. One who said that he liked the silent church before the service begins better than any sermon could hardly be expected to gain the full approval of men whose business it is to preach. His proclamation and practice of self-reliance was and always will be appalling to traditionalists of every hue. He went to original sources rather than to the commentaries.

"I know what say the fathers wise,
    The Book itself before me lies," . . .

It was not the Bible alone, but the Book of Nature and of Life.

Men who wear the outer garments of religious

and social respectability but are only faintly warmed by inner fires have ever been abashed by such fearless originality. But the contact of any soul with God is always an original experience, bearing its own authority, and every honest historian of the human spirit must honor one who objected to the current practice of Christianity chiefly because he believed that it neglected the soul.

The angelic quality in Emerson was perceived by Carlyle and others; and until this day the memory of this dreamy but indomitable man who once roamed the meadows and woodlands of quiet Concord remains as a benediction. Though to outward appearance he was dry and chill, surely there are few figures in the literary history of any land of whom it may be more truly said that spiritual emotions were the habitual center of personal energy; and perhaps there is nowhere in our literary heritage a nobler challenge to spiritual integrity and unconquerable courage. Not because he was Emerson, but because he regarded himself as a man created in the image of God and assumed with regnant confidence the prerogatives of humanity, could he say that he was the heir of all nature and all history.

"I am the owner of the sphere,
    Of the seven stars and the solar year,

Of Caesar's hand, and Plato's brain,
Of Lord Christ's heart, and Shakespeare's
strain."

This is more than angelic: it is Godlike.

Whatever there may be of universality in Emerson's stirring message, and he thought there was much, his personal life, like that of Thoreau, was voluntarily withdrawn and cloistered. His saintliness received no baptism of fire and blood on the battlefield, as did that of Lee and Jackson; from the compromises of politics which, in his opinion, enmeshed Daniel Webster, he was far removed; with the cruel strife and crass materialism of the market place he had nothing at all to do. His animal spirits, he said, were low; and he could hardly have endured the physical hardships of the Western trail. This pioneer of the spirit chose what seemed to him the better way, for him the only way, but it was a woodland path for an individual not a highway for society, and his countrymen have not been content to loiter in it while a continent awaited conquest and exploitation. Has saintliness appeared at all among these Americans of more ruthless nature who have faced immediate problems and perils of a cruder sort?

That this or any other continent was conquered, cleared, and peopled in the spirit of

Christian compassion, no sensible man can claim. The march of the pioneers was heroic, magnificent, but it partook of the cruelty of nature and often surpassed that of the savages by whom it was opposed. Our physical triumphs were achieved by character of the sterner sort, by intelligence, and by force; no more than in the international strife of European peoples were victories won by love and chivalry. It is not for the moralist to claim that they could have been.

However, it may be pointed out in passing that there are highlights in even so dark a picture as that of American relations with the hapless Indians. From the days of John Eliot in Massachusetts to those of Bishop Henry B. Whipple in Minnesota and Bishop William Hobart Hare, "Apostle to the Sioux," there were those who had compassion on the "red children of God," as there are today in the Indian Bureau. The first Bible printed in North America was Eliot's translation into the Indian language, now a treasure to collectors, and the belated reform of the Indian Service after the Civil War followed the lines suggested by the Episcopal bishop of Minnesota, who had viewed cruelty and massacre at first hand in his frontier diocese. These men did not compose the strife of an imperfect world, but they sought to temper its excesses, and, though relatively obscure in history, they appear to the close observer as active saints in a field of great personal danger.

The exploitation of the continent, no less than its physical conquest, has been marked by ruthless aggressiveness rather than Christian selflessness. Some of our financiers have been colossal in historic stature, as they have surpassed Croesus in opulence, but few of them qualify for the gallery of saints. It has always been characteristic of our society, and nowhere more than among the Puritans, to glorify the economic virtues, such as industry and thrift, rather than the social virtues, such as charity and compassion; and financial success has not infrequently been regarded as an evidence of divine approval. But before the day of Andrew Carnegie and John D. Rockefeller, many a prosperous layman asked himself the question which Lewis Tappan, a generous contributor to the cause of Abolition, embodied in a pamphlet, "Is It Right to Be Rich?" The sense of stewardship has played no small part in the magnificent story of American philanthropy, but we cannot assign to these donors a crown of sanctity which they have rarely claimed for themselves.

American society has bred its quota of picturesque buccaneers, who in spirit sailed beneath the skull and crossbones rather than the cross.

Not even Captain Kidd is a more colorful figure in the annals of piracy than Charles W. Morse, once of the state of Maine, later of New York and of the Atlanta penitentiary, whence he emerged under conditions suggestive of comic opera to indulge in further incredible depredations. It would be extravagant to claim that in the history of American finance Morse's career is symbolical, but perhaps "Golden Rule" Nash was no more typical of his generation of business men. This former Seventh-Day Adventist, who was also at times a minister of the Disciples of Christ, a hobo, a plasterer, and a salesman, ultimately became a manufacturer of men's clothing in Cincinnati. Becoming convinced that the kingdom of God could be established on earth only by the literal application of the Golden Rule, he advanced the wages of his men at a time when his balance sheet was in the red and early liquidation seemed inevitable. Far from declining, however, his business grew by leaps and bounds. History affords few better examples of the happy combination of prosperity and humanity, or of shrewd business judgment with evangelical zeal. Nash died before the depression, and the kingdom of God is not yet triumphant on earth, but he may be presented as a strong candidate for canonization.

Candidates for sainthood of an unconventional

type can also be brought forward by historians of
the movements of labor. It is unlikely that one
of these will be Bill Haywood of the I.W.W.,
who was charged with complicity in the assassi-
nation of the governor of Idaho, though not convicted, and was a storm center of industrial warfare for a generation. Finally, during the World
War, he was convicted of sedition and fled to
Soviet Russia, where he died in obscurity. His
rejection as a candidate for sainthood even by
labor partisans would not be because of his failure
to attend church after he was ten, but because of
his ultimate repudiation by his own group and
because in retrospect his violence appears to have
been unrelieved by spirituality. A much more
likely subject is John Mitchell, president of the
United Mine Workers of America during the
successful anthracite strike of 1902, whose conduct in the conference room seemed to President
Theodore Roosevelt more gentlemanly than that
of the operators by whom he was so bitterly
opposed. This amazingly serene leader of an unpopular cause was brought up by devout Presbyterians, ultimately turned Catholic, and commonly wore a long black coat of ministerial cut.
To innumerable workingmen who have heard
his story he doubtless appears as one of Labor's
saints. Also, there was Mother (Mary Harris)
Jones, a little Irishwoman, who lost her husband

and children in a yellow-fever epidemic in Memphis, Tennessee, and all her worldly goods in the famous Chicago fire, and afterward submerged her life in the cause of working people. Her black bonnet was a familiar sight for half a century in scenes of industrial strife, and on her one hundredth birthday this fiery but beloved agitator received congratulations, among others, from John D. Rockefeller, Jr.

As the rich pageant of our social history passes in review innumerable contrasts appear. If there was brilliant worldly cynicism on the *New York Sun* under Charles A. Dana, there was moral fervor in the *New York Tribune* under Horace Greeley. The latter journalist, whose earlier violence against slavery did not prevent his offering bail for the imprisoned Jefferson Davis, undoubtedly was regarded by many of his followers as an oracle and a sort of bewhiskered saint, but to others he seemed merely eccentric. Behind the mighty ax of Carry Nation, smasher of plate-glass and furniture in saloons, were 175 pounds of physical power and, in the opinion of others besides the saloonkeepers, many more pounds of madness; but Dorothea Dix, gentle, timid, and soft-spoken, in her long struggle to secure hospitals for the insane, was "driven by the white heat of compassion." There can be no question here, I think, which was the fanatic and

which the saint. Senator Vardaman of Missis-
sippi, clad in white and drawn by a team of white
oxen, inveighed against the "menace" of Negro
education before a rural constituency, and, by
making himself the beneficiary of inflamed prejudice, gained political preferment; while Booker
T. Washington of Alabama, whose skin was
brown, patiently taught members of a backward
race to be better workmen and thus to advance
the civilization of which both Negroes and whites
are inseparable parts. Here, demagoguery and
passion confronted humanity and common sense.

It taxes the power of the historian even to
depict the variegated American scene and the
actors upon it; and he is loath to assume the rôle
of censor. Who knows how many villains have
knifed their victims secretly, how many spiritual
flowers have bloomed unseen, how many martyrs
have been stoned in obscurity? In our ignorance
and incompetence we can only hope and believe
that somewhere in the universe truth is known
and justice is accorded.

For the purposes of these modest lectures it
seems wisest to begin, not with controversial
figures in public life, whose godliness is suspect,
or with soldiers whose business it is to kill; not
with the heroes of literature whose individualism
so often borders on egoism, or with any of the
representatives of miscellaneous groups to whom

a degree of saintliness will not be readily accorded. For reasons of prudence, if for no other, we shall start with those who have assumed a definite religious vocation, of which it may be hoped that they were worthy. We shall begin with the clergy.

To this group alone, extraordinarily diverse in a land where sects have been free to flourish and multiply, a whole series of lectures and of books could easily be devoted. But, as life in America until relatively recent times has not flowed in sharply defined professional channels, and ministers have not generally been separated from the encompassing world even by their dress, saintliness has often been without benefit of ordination. Clergymen themselves have not only administered colleges, universities, and foundations, but have founded and ruled towns and commonwealths; while certain laymen, in a vast variety of occupations, have been dominated by a zeal which can be characterized only as religious. As the wind bloweth, the Spirit moveth where it listeth.

The attempt to single from the multitude individuals who seem worthy of a halo is perilous; and, in order to avoid chaos, we shall assemble them in major groups that are not commonly associated with exploitation or self-aggrandizement. We shall try to deal with groups and persons whose background has been unquestionably religious, even though at a later time the ecclesiastical tie may have become attenuated or been actually severed. After the clergy, we shall deal with reformers of crusading zeal, like the Abolitionists, even though some of them became pitiless in the cause of mercy; and with women who have won glory in classroom, forum, and settlement. We shall speak of educators who had the spirit of missionaries and evangelists and were subject to the same danger of subordinating intelligence to emotion. Finally, we shall talk of scholars in whom the light of learning has burned clear, even though it may have lost the warmth it had in the hearts and minds of cruder men. Somewhere in the roster we shall find reformers who have remembered to be merciful; evangelists of popular education who have maintained high intelligence; scholars who have not forgotten humanity in their quest of elusive truth. In men and women like these, whether or not we call them saints, has always lain the hope of a befogged and uncertain world.

II

THE CLERGY IN AMERICAN
ACHIEVEMENT

IN entering upon a discussion of the achievements of saints as viewed in the light of history, I am fully aware of dangers and valid criti-
cisms. Few religious people will accept as final
any worldly judgment on the accomplishments
of any saint. Least of all men can men of God be
graded mechanically by the number of columns
devoted to them in the newspapers, by the ephem-
eral popularity or notoriety which they may
gain, by the number of dollars they collect or
contribute, even by a count of the souls they saved
—if such a count were possible. Only a Supreme
Intelligence can measure their harvest and
assess its quality.

Nonetheless, historical judgments upon men
who may have regarded themselves as citizens of
another world are not without significance. Hitler and his satellites may place little value, except
nuisance value, on Pastor Niemöller and Cardinal Innitzer, but the present rulers of Germany
do not comprise the supreme court of history.
Even granting as one must grant that opinions
about institutions, ecclesiastical as well as secular,

vary from age to age, the spiritual heroes of the world remain its greatest heroes, and they have left on the pages of history an impress more indelible than that of any military conqueror. It is not necessary to enter Saint Peter's celestial domain or to seek a grand jury of archangels to procure such a judgment. As William James has said, the greatest saints need but show themselves, and their stature is recognized without question. Besides Saint Francis and Martin Luther, Ignatius Loyola and John Wesley, Dwight L. Moody and Phillips Brooks, he said, "the strong men of this world and no other seem as dry as sticks, as hard and crude as blocks of stone or brickbats."[1] Of lesser men, of course, even posterity is more uncertain, frequently because so few of the facts are known. All too often, we see through a glass darkly.

It is my purpose here to survey selected groups from the past American scene, beginning with the clergymen, and to essay some comments on their historic achievements and importance. No infallible criterion can be applied and no claim will be made by this particular judge to membership in any supreme court of history. However, I will avail myself of the collective judgments that are embodied in the *Dictionary of*

---

[1] *The Varieties of Religious Experience,* p. 376.

American Biography, and will state some of
them in bald and formidable statistics.

Of the 13,633 persons included in the *Dictionary* about 1,900 were clergymen. It is impossible to give exact figures because of the
variety of classifications. There are persons
designated as clergymen, bishops, missionaries,
theologians, educators, and religious leaders.
There is duplication in almost every list, and
often it is impossible to decide what the major
occupation was. Clergymen have complicated
matters further by engaging in other than religious pursuits. An approximate figure, therefore, will have to serve. We will say, then, that
clergymen comprise about fourteen per cent of
the whole, or almost one out of seven. In *Appletons' Cyclopaedia of American Biography*,
published a generation earlier, the percentage is
slightly higher, being about sixteen per cent. It
might be argued that there was a corresponding
decline in the importance of the clergy in American life during the intervening generation, but
the circumstances under which the two works
were compiled were not identical and no such
mechanical comparison can properly be made.
That there has been a decline in recent years will
be generally agreed, I believe, but not even the
later work covers the last generation adequately,
and for this reason, if for no other, statistical

support for such a generalization would have to be found elsewhere.

Limiting ourselves to the *Dictionary* and the period covered by it, we can make significant comparisons with other groups. The clergy are exceeded in number by only two other groups: state and federal officials, whom we ordinarily term statesmen; and writers, including editors. Officers of the army and navy are considerably less numerous than clergymen, even though, in the United States, many of the former were not in a strict sense professional military or naval men and gained part of their fame in other fields of endeavor. Business men, artists, engineers, inventors, and all other major groups suffer by comparison with the clerical body as a whole.

Various explanations can be given for the large number of clergymen who have achieved eminence in America. For one thing, we have had, and still have, an extraordinarily large number of sects in the United States, and the pioneer figures in connection with them are of definite historical interest. Furthermore, many ministers have engaged in other activities which have given them prominence. Whatever explanations may be given, the statistics are distinctly impressive. Comparisons with other countries are practically impossible because of the lack of comparable information and statistics, but it is entirely safe to say that clergymen have played a very conspicuous part in American history and that the churches have made exceedingly distinguished contributions to American achievement. Whatever may be said of the present or the future, the record of the past cannot be successfully assailed. Despite their earlier emphasis on politics and their more recent emphasis on economics, few historians will be disposed to assail it. A general historical impression is strengthened by these biographical statistics.

Our emphasis here is on men, not on the churches or the sects which they served, but a breakdown of the figures into denominational categories is not without interest. It is difficult to prove anything by gross statistics about the relative influence of different denominations in American life. It is not sufficient to count the noses of their distinguished men. The element of time is of prime importance in making comparisons. Because Henry Cabot Lodge ignored this factor when he wrote his well-known essay, "The Distribution of Ability in the United States," he erred in certain of his generalizations about the geographical distribution of notable Americans.[2] Obviously, one cannot compare the

---

[2] See his *Historical and Political Essays* (1892); and my own article, "The Geography of American Achievement," *Atlantic Monthly*, December, 1934.

gross figures for Massachusetts and Iowa, for the former commonwealth has had a much longer history. Similar allowance must be made for the fact that Congregationalism began with the first settlement in New England, while the history of American Methodism did not begin until the decade before the Revolution. The number of adherents of a particular denominational group is an equally important factor. During the same period of time Delaware could not be expected to produce as many distinguished men as New York, or the small Unitarian group as many as the large body of Roman Catholics. Finally, even if unexceptionable statistics could be compiled—and they cannot be—they would be proof, not of the influence of a particular denomination on society, but of its productiveness of distinguished individuals. One would expect a great church to produce great men, but there are other indexes of the influence and achievements of any religious group.

For these reasons a breakdown of the gross figures along denominational lines may be inconclusive, but it is interesting. Upon the face of the figures, the sects which have produced distinguished men most abundantly are the Anglican-Episcopalians, the Congregationalists, and the Presbyterians. The Roman Catholics comprise an intermediate group between these and the Methodists and Baptists. The Unitarians rank lower still in the aggregate, but the number of adherents has been so small that no proper comparisons can be made. In proportion to their numbers their achievements may be the most notable of all. The time element is favorable to the Anglican-Episcopal group and to the Congregationalists, but the distinction of their representatives in the nineteenth century is out of all proportion to the membership of their churches during that period. Until the Revolution there were few Methodists in the country, and until the nineteenth century few Catholics, but in recent generations they have been most numerous of all.

If these figures should seem confusing as well as inconclusive, it may be that more fruitful generalizations can be based on an analysis of a smaller and more distinguished sample. The qualitative standard can then be applied. Unfortunately, however, quality and distinction are not susceptible of exact measurement. As an editor it was my task, in co-operation with others, to assign to various individuals the amount of space which their achievements and importance seemed to deserve. Our imperfect judgments are certainly not defensible in detail, but the presumption is that a man who was assigned 5,000 words by the editors was more important than a man to whom 500 words were allotted. Roughly speaking, historical importance was measured, and it is to be hoped that justice was approximated.

Finding it impossible to analyze the careers of the 1,900 clergymen in the *Dictionary of American Biography*, I set an arbitrary boundary line at two columns, or somewhat less than 1,000 words, and made a list of all the clergymen whose biographies occupy that much space or more. It appeared that there were nearly 300 of them. Dividing these names among the various denominational groups, one arrives at the following percentages:

1. Congregationalists   20%
2. Anglican-Episcopalians   16%
3. Presbyterians   14%
4. Roman Catholics   12%
5. Methodists   9%
6. Unitarians   7%
7. Baptists   6%
8. Lutherans   5%
   Others   11%

This analysis strengthens the general conclusions based on larger numbers, though there is some variation in the order of the denominations. In this selected group the Congregationalists take first place and the Unitarians rise above the Baptists. The other denominations occupy the same relative position.

Students of biography, however, are interested in persons rather than statistics. We want to talk about figures on the stage of action, not figures on a statistical chart. Accordingly, we prefer to deal with a much smaller group, susceptible of more detailed analysis. Can we not choose a clerical Hall of Fame and examine individual careers more closely? There is no likelihood, of course, that any selection will merit or receive universal approval. Despite the perils that are involved, I have drawn up a list of twenty-five, on the mechanical basis of the space allotted them in the *Dictionary of American Biography*, exercising personal discretion only in choosing between a few names at the bottom of the list where biographies are of practically the same length. Also, I have arbitrarily excluded a few clergymen, generally in the recent period, whose careers were essentially nonecclesiastical, and have included one eminent religious leader who was not ordained. It would be inappropriate, I think, to include William Graham Sumner, even though he was ordained, or to exclude Dwight L. Moody because he was not.

For purposes of convenience we will first list these clerical immortals in denominational classes. Since no fewer than eight of the twenty-five, including some who would receive the vote of almost every informed elector, were Congregationalists, we can appropriately begin with them.

CONGREGATIONALISTS

Jonathan Edwards. Few will question the primacy of this initiator of the Great Awakening who has so long been regarded as the major saint of New England Calvinism and the most noted of American theologians. Repelled though men now may be by the pitilessness of his logic, time has served but to increase respect for the extraordinary powers of his mind and the rare spiritual beauty of his life.

Henry Ward Beecher. Despite the unfavorable publicity which was given to one episode in the personal life of this famous preacher and reformer, his conspicuous leadership in public life during his generation remains unquestionable; and his personality still appears robust and colorful.

Horace Bushnell. Some will prefer the apostle of Christian nurture to the orator of Plymouth Church. Emphasizing religious experience rather than cold logic, Bushnell brought to an end the theological movement which began with Jonathan Edwards and inaugurated another that was more in accord with human nature.

Increase Mather. He was the first Puritan of his generation in Massachusetts, at a time when clergymen were often embroiled in political controversy and were powers in affairs of state.

Cotton Mather. The son of Increase Mather and grandson of John Cotton, he was relatively unsuccessful as a politician and unlovable as a person, but was eminent in his generation and still commands respect for his scholarship.

Timothy Dwight. This grandson of Jonathan Edwards was probably the most famous president of Yale. The dominance of his position in church, school, and state, caused him to be called "the Pope." An embodiment of stubborn Federalism, perhaps he represents conservative Connecticut Congregationalism at its best.

Dwight L. Moody. The greatest of American-born evangelists, he represents neither the intellectualism nor the clericalism of New England, but its sanctified common sense. In him evangelism was without taint of commercialism or exhibitionism.

Ezra Stiles. Another president of Yale, he was eminent as a clergyman and even more notable for his learning and his leadership in education.

To this impressive list other important names might easily be added, such as John Cotton, Thomas Hooker, John Davenport, and Leonard Bacon. No one of these men seems to have been of equal stature with the eight who are named above, but one or more of them may be preferred by some students to certain of the lesser figures from other sects who are named below.   In connection with the Congregationalists one is embarrassed by riches.

UNITARIANS

From the Congregational tradition stemmed the Unitarian, which is here represented by two famous names.

William Ellery Channing.   More than any other single individual he was the founder of American Unitarianism, although he himself was essentially unsectarian in spirit.   His influence was felt in literature and reform, but he will doubtless be best remembered by the inscription beneath his statue in Boston: "He breathed into theology a humane spirit."

Theodore Parker.   Also notable as a writer and reformer, he is most memorable as a theologian who sought a science of religion, based on experience.

PRESBYTERIANS

The Presbyterians, brothers of the Congregationalists in doctrine, though less influenced by the liberalizing influence of the nineteenth century, have two representatives.

John Witherspoon.   This Scotch-born president of the College of New Jersey (Princeton) was also a signer of the Declaration of Independence. His prominence was partly political, but this democratic conservative became a dominant figure in American Presbyterianism.

Gilbert Tennent. The Irish-born son of the founder of the "Log College," represented evangelism rather than intellectuality. He shared with George Whitefield and Jonathan Edwards the leadership of the Great Awakening.

Had this list been extended beyond twenty-five, place should have been found on it for Charles G. Finney, the revivalist. In preparing the way for the antislavery crusaders, and in his long service to Oberlin College, he won for himself a notable place in the history of reform and of religious education. However, the Congregationalists also can claim him, for during the latter years of his life he was identified with them. Some Presbyterians, in their turn, will probably claim Jonathan Edwards.

EPISCOPALIANS

Like the Presbyterians, the Anglican-Episcopal group is more largely represented on the longer list of notable clergymen than in this group of the most eminent. Two names are included here.

Phillips Brooks. He clearly belongs among

the immortals and that not because of reform
activities, as in the case of Henry Ward Beecher,
or because of his official position, for his election
to the bishopric came late in life and was merely
an incident in his career.   His fame was that of a
preacher; his genius was neither political nor
ecclesiastical, but spiritual.   The essential elements of preaching, he said, are truth and personality.   However doubtful men may have been
of truth, they were slow to question it when they
saw it embodied in such a rich and harmonious
personality.

William Smith.   The first provost of the College, Academy, and Charitable School of Philadelphia, whence the University of Pennsylvania
emerged, serves as a striking contrast. He did
conspicuous service to the cause of education, and
his ecclesiastical eminence might well have
caused him to be appointed the first Anglican
bishop in America had there been one. His abilities and services make it impossible to disregard
him, but his distinction was rather that of a man
of affairs than of a spiritual leader.

METHODISTS

If we include among them one who was and
remained an Englishman and had only a part of
his famous career on this continent, the Methodists have three representatives.

George Whitefield. The most dynamic force in the Great Awakening cannot well be omitted from any American list, even though he also belongs to English history. Essentially emotional where Jonathan Edwards was intellectual, he is perhaps the only figure in American religious history who can be compared in influence with the somber theologian of Northampton, and in the effectiveness of his religious oratory he ranks among the greatest of all ages.

Francis Asbury. If not the founder of American Methodism, he was its head during the first generation of its separate existence and its chief organizer. Autocratic in method, he was the prince of a democratic church; indefatigable in his zeal, he was the greatest of an heroic line of circuit riders.

Jesse Lee. Second only to Asbury in the establishment of Methodism, he was its first American historian. Born in Virginia, he won fame chiefly for his labors in New England. Big in body and in spirit, he was thought too jovial and too independent to be a bishop, but he exemplifies as few others have done the heartiness of evangelical ism.

Roman Catholics

Second in number only to the Congregationalists are the Catholics. The five men named below were all high ecclesiastics and three of them were born abroad; but the greatest of them, in the opinion of an outsider, were notable exponents of Americanism.

John Ireland. Born in Ireland, he served as a chaplain in the Union Army, and while a pastor in Saint Paul was an implacable foe of political corruption and the liquor interests. As Archbishop of Saint Paul he dominated his province and remained a powerful factor in public affairs. He opposed the movement for the appointment of racial bishops in the United States and the consequent perpetuation of racial lines, was notable in his church for his friendliness toward the public schools, and advocated teaching in English in the parochial schools. Honored by Catholics for his distinguished services to his church, he may be honored by all Americans for his devotion to his country.

James Cardinal Gibbons. He was born in Baltimore and, though brought up as a boy in Ireland, is associated chiefly with the city of his birth. More active even than Archbishop Ireland in the establishment and development of the Catholic University of America, he was equally notable for his staunch Americanism.

John Joseph Hughes. This Archbishop of New York was most notable for his championship of his church, the Irish, and the parochial schools at a time when they faced powerful opposition.

John England. This incorrigible Irish democrat gained his fame as the Bishop of Charleston, in a small diocese untouched by the tides of immigration. In his church, in America as in Ireland, he fought valiantly for democracy.

John Carroll. This native of Maryland, who was the first Catholic bishop in America and the first archbishop of Baltimore, was the chief organizer of his church in America after the Revolution.

OTHER DENOMINATIONS

No other church has more than one representative on this list. For the Baptists, we have Isaac Backus, pastor for fifty years in Middleboro, Massachusetts, and the chief itinerant missionary of his group, especially in New England. His significance consists chiefly in his championship of religious liberty and of democratic church government and in his work as a church historian.

The Disciples of Christ are represented by Alexander Campbell, the nonsectarian who was the chief founder of this sect. Born of a Scotch family in Ireland, he came under Presbyterian influences in early life, but was later associated with the Baptists. The Universalists are represented by their founder in America, John Murray, who was born in England and greatly affected by Wesley and Whitefield. Like so many others, he had his chief career in New England.

On this select list there is no individual Lutheran figure. Mention should be made, however, of a notable family group, the Muhlenbergs, who contributed four Lutheran clergymen of more than ordinary distinction and one Episcopalian. There is no Jewish figure, but reference may be made at least to Rabbi Isaac M. Wise of Cincinnati, the greatest figure in Reformed Judaism in his generation and notable as an advocate of Americanism.

It would be easy for somebody else to compile an equally acceptable list of twenty-five that would contain more names from groups that are sparsely represented here. The numerical distribution along denominational lines cannot be defended in detail. However, the extraordinary prominence of the Congregationalists, with whom the Unitarians may properly be associated, cannot be overlooked. In my opinion, this group would bulk large on any lists that historians might compile. The figures are the more significant because they strengthen impressions gained from the consideration of larger numbers. All indexes are favorable to this group.

Various explanations of Congregational eminence in American religious history can be given.

(1) It may be said that their form of government has tended to develop outstanding pastors and to emphasize their importance as individuals. This argument, however, applies equally to the Baptists, whose form of church government has been essentially the same. On the other hand, it may be argued that the hierarchical structure of the Catholic Church has tended to give the prelates an importance far beyond what they would have had as pastors in a more individualistic organization. Among Methodists, also, a bishop has had importance and prominence because of the office that he holds. It is worthy of note, however, that the founders of Methodism, who were independent of its ecclesiasticism or were the creators of it, were greater men than their successors in the formal episcopacy. No bishop of a later time can properly be compared with Wesley, Whitefield, or Asbury. It is difficult to draw a valid generalization from all this confusion, but at least it must be clear that Congregational eminence cannot be explained entirely or primarily as the result of the form of government.

(2) The intellectual tradition of the Congregational Church has long seemed to many people a partial explanation of its eminence. Pastors were men of learning and even thinkers in their own right. Jonathan Edwards was not merely

a preacher of power, but one of the great intellects of his time. The number of books that have been written by ministers of his faith is extraordinary, not to say appalling. Even if it be true that most of them are now of antiquarian interest only, the showing is remarkable. The comparison with other sects in this respect is all in favor of the Congregationalists, and it is no accident that the colleges and universities founded by them have become famous throughout the civilized world. Never content with sheer emotionalism, as the evangelicals have so often been, they wedded mind and spirit. Their intellectuality may frequently have been cold and barren, but as historically manifested it commands and deserves profound respect. Apart from the Unitarians, the other religious group that is most comparable with the Congregationalists in this respect consists of the Presbyterians, who have produced almost as many men of moderate distinction but considerably fewer of the highest eminence. One reason for this may be that Presbyterianism was less affected by the liberalizing movements of thought in the nineteenth century. From the rigid shell of Calvinism the Congregationalists emerged earlier. However, the eminence of their clergy cannot be explained on this ground alone.

(3) It may be argued that the close union of Church and State in New England, making her

clergy powerful in public affairs, gave them a prominence which clergymen elsewhere did not often gain. This is unquestionable, I think, but many of the greatest Congregational figures belong in a later period, when the political ties were broken. Even if clergymen who were prominent in affairs of State be eliminated—the Mathers and Timothy Dwight, for instance—there remain Jonathan Edwards, Horace Bushnell, Dwight L. Moody, and others who labored in the religious rather than the political vineyard.

(4) The most important reason, including all others, is that the Congregationalists came from New England and chiefly labored there. Exaggerated claims have often been made for the rôle of this section in American history and American life. In the field of government, in particular, it has been greatly overrated. Virginia was far more important in the first generation of the republic and New York is at the present time. But the historic pre-eminence of New England as a source of religious leadership cannot be questioned. This list of eminent religious figures bears eloquent testimony to the truth of this statement, for no fewer than twelve of the total of twenty-five, and of the twenty Protestants, were born there. The New Englanders include not merely the Congregationalists and Unitarians, but also Phillips Brooks, greatest of

the Episcopalians, and Isaac Backus, the sole
representative of the Baptists. It may also be
remarked that Mary Baker Eddy, the mother of
Christian Science, and Joseph Smith and Brig-
ham Young, the founders of Mormonism, were
born in New England. Except for Henry Ward
Beecher, all of these twelve men from our list of
twenty-five had their careers chiefly in New England, as also had Jesse Lee, the Methodist, and
John Murray, the Universalist.

The relative backwardness of other sections in
producing eminent native clergymen is made
clear by a further geographical analysis of this
list of twenty-five. No native clergyman of the
first rank has yet come out of New York, New
Jersey, or Pennsylvania, though it cannot be
claimed that these states have not had time to
produce them. Maryland is represented by two
Roman Catholics; Virginia, with her incomparable galaxy of statesmen and soldiers, contributed only the Methodist Jesse Lee; and the
other Southern states are entirely without repre-
sentation.

No one of these twenty-five great names belongs to the American West. The explanation
of this apparent backwardness, however, together
with that of the newer states of the South, is inseparable from a consideration of chronological
periods and the historic forces operating within

them. Whether or not it be true that when the
sons of the newer American states arrived at
maturity the creative age of American Christianity, and especially of American Protestantism
was past, it is true that the latest from our list
of eminent clergymen was born a hundred years
ago. Unless the addition of the names of men
now living should change the chronological proportions of the list, we may presume that during
recent generations, when men of western birth
have played so great a part in national life, the
times have not been propitious for religious leadership of the first order. The explanation for
the backwardness, at an earlier time, of all
regions except New England seems to be the
closeness of the tie with the Mother Country and
the dependence on her for leadership.

No fewer than ten of these twenty-five emi-
nent clergymen were born in the British Isles.
George Whitefield came from England and re-
turned thither. From England also came the
Methodist Francis Asbury, the Anglican Wil-
liam Smith, and the Universalist John Murray.
From Ireland came three Catholic prelates—
John Ireland, John Joseph Hughes, and John
England; Alexander Campbell, of the Disciples
of Christ; and Gilbert Tennent of the Presbyter-
ians. Scotland contributed the Presbyterian John
Witherspoon. It seems clear from these facts

alone that New England declared religious independence of the mother country and developed native leadership much earlier than any
other region; and that all other churches besides
those in New England were to a notable extent
dependent on leadership from abroad.

For purposes of interpretation it seems desirable, finally, to consider the chronological periods
in which these twenty-five immortals lived.
They may be divided into four groups: a colonial
group, whose careers occurred before 1765; and
three others, each falling within a period of fifty
years — 1765-1815, 1815-1865, 1865-1915.
The earliest birthdate is that of Increase Mather
in 1639; and the latest deathdate is that of Cardinal Gibbons in 1921.

The colonial group consists of leaders in
Church and State in New England, that is, the
two Mathers; and of men associated with the
Great Awakening about the middle of the eighteenth century, Jonathan Edwards, George
Whitefield, Gilbert Tennent, and Isaac Backus,
though the career of the last of these carried over
into the next period.

The second group (1765-1815) contains pioneers in the establishment of denominations:
Francis Asbury and Jesse Lee for the Methodists, Isaac Backus for the Baptists, and John Mur-

ray for the Universalists; and clerical leaders in
education, like John Witherspoon of Princeton,
William Smith of Philadelphia, Ezra Stiles and
Timothy Dwight of Yale.

The third group (1815-1865) also contains
founders and pioneers—Archbishop Carroll,
Archbishop Hughes, and Bishop England in the
growing Catholic Church; Alexander Campbell
of the Disciples of Christ; William Ellery Channing and Theodore Parker of the Unitarians.
These two men were also engaged in reform, as
was Henry Ward Beecher in the days of Abolitionism, and were concerned with theology as
Horace Bushnell was.

The fourth group (1865-1915) includes
Beecher and Bushnell again, for they lived on.
The others were powerful Catholic prelates in a
period of enormous growth as the result of immigration, Archbishop Ireland and Cardinal Gibbons; the incomparable rector of a great Boston
parish, Phillips Brooks; and Dwight L. Moody,
the most vital recent figure in Congregationalism,
now grown free and tolerant but moribund. For
all of them, except perhaps John Ireland in
Minnesota, the pioneering age was past. The
others lived in an autumn season, when men
gather harvests which other men have sowed.
Even the evangelism of Moody was of the set-
tled community, not the frontier.

It would be improper to remark that after them the winter came, when clergymen, like other people, sit comfortably at home; but I think it is correct to say that no one replaced these giants of autumn when they disappeared. Phillips Brooks died, all too soon, in 1893; and Dwight L. Moody, two years his junior, ended his days near the close of the century. The two great prelates lived to riper age, into the new era of World War, which brought to no one either victory or peace. But these last giants of a confident Christianity, Brooks, Moody, Ireland, Gibbons, considerably antedated the Civil War. All were born in the 1830's, were educated before the great sectional conflict, and had their careers thereafter.

Without improper reference to living men, whom we are not considering here, I will venture the sad statement that no religious leader of comparable historic stature grew to manhood in the materialistic era which followed our Civil War. Whether the fault was with the men or the times I shall not here attempt to say. But I will venture to assert that the clergymen of America, bewildered for half a century by industrialism and baffled by the slums, have heard in our own day a clarion call to heroism beyond anything that the circuit rider ever knew. In these dark days of violence and fear and hatred the souls of brave men are being tempered for battles that are to come. Who knows but that even in this blessed land there may be martyrs, that champions will here answer the challenge, and that apostles will appear.

III

CRUSADERS OF REFORM

REFORMERS cannot be readily segregated from any list of notables, as clergymen can, for they do not constitute a distinct calling. There have been and still are men and women who may properly be described as "professional" reformers; yet they do not enter this profession through the door of ordination as clergymen do, though some of them are clergymen; they are not admitted to it as lawyers are to the bar, though some of them are lawyers. Clearly, they are professionals whenever the advocacy of some sort of reform is their occupation and provides their means of livelihood, modest though that livelihood may be. Here, as elsewhere, the laborer may be worthy of his hire, but the public is rather suspicious of this group, as it is of paid lobbyists of any sort. The term "professional" may also be applied less exactly to men and women, supported in some other way and nominally engaged in some other sort of activity, who nonetheless find in the advocacy of reform a continuing and absorbing avocation. Wendell Phillips, who was wealthy as well as aristocratic, did not need to depend on his nominal profession as a lawyer: his life was given rather to agitation for unfriended causes, like Abolition, which he deemed righteous and from which abuse was his chief return.

At the other extreme are those whose advocacy of some special reform or reforms is incidental to a larger task. A general who assumes command of an army, or a cabinet officer who takes charge of a department of the government, may deem it necessary to "reform" its administration. People who leave things just as they are because of timidity or indolence are generally ineffective. Strong men nearly always change something. In a sense, Charles W. Eliot was a reformer in education, as was Theodore Roosevelt in public life, but we properly designate these men as statesmen in their respective fields. The main task of one of them was to direct a university, of the other to govern a nation. Such men often effect changes that are too far-reaching to be called incidental, and they themselves cannot be described as amateurs, but they were not professional reformers. Harvey W. Wiley, as chief chemist of the United States Department of Agriculture, thought it necessary to launch a crusade against impure food and was often called a reformer. Whether or not the term is accurate in this case depends upon the emphasis which may be perceived in his career as a whole.

The objectives of reform are as varied as the advocates. Some clamor for pure food, others for the conservation of natural resources or the improvement of the Civil Service. Feminists like Susan B. Anthony have agitated for woman's suffrage, while Jacob A. Riis strove to improve conditions in the slums. Henry George advocated the reform of economic life by the institution of a single tax on land, while John Humphrey Noyes established the most successful of American Utopias in the Oneida Community in New York. A common denominator for these diverse personalities, if not for their objectives, might be found in their earnestness, but we shall not seek it here.

For our more restricted purposes, it will be unnecessary to describe the part played by religious men and women in political and social reform in America. Indeed, it would be impossible to do so. Suffice it to say that to vigorous men and women of a religious nature reform activity of one sort or another is a very natural thing, all the more, perhaps, if they are not engaged professionally in the offices of the church and must express themselves in some external way. Whether they wear the cloth or not, strong men require an outlet for their moral energy and are more likely than weak men to rush into battle. In a dynamic society the active religious spirit does not flee the world and cultivate flowers of contemplation, but endeavors in some way to advance the kingdom of God on earth.

Our primary concern here will be with men who conceived of themselves as moral crusaders and claimed religious sanction for the reforms they championed. The changes which they advocated may have had important political and social implications, but these have often been minimized through excess of moral zeal, and sometimes the consequences have been unfortunate. The issue is often oversimplified by the reformer who regards his cause as moral, and it is made to appear a clearcut question of right or wrong. Herein lies his chief weakness and his greatest strength.

"The only straight line in Nature that I remember," said Emerson in 1843, "is the spider swinging down from a twig." Following the line of thought suggested by the Concord sage, we may say that nature does not express herself in geometric figures: they are abstractions, created by the minds of men. Carrying the analogy a step further, one may say that of all men who deal with human and social phenomena, moral reformers are among those who are most prone to the abstractions that are symbolized by geometry. Life must follow a straight line, they think, without deviation; society should restrain itself

within the confines of a rectangle. Men of affairs,
engaged in business or politics, have long since
learned—indeed, some of them have learned
far too well—that they must be content with
approximations of geometric perfection. Without straining a figure of speech, one can say on
the basis of common observation that often there
is a formidable and forbidding angularity of
mind among reformers, whereas the minds of
most men may be symbolized by lines that sometimes break and often curve or bend. No wonder
that to the artistic temperament the angular reformer is anathema. To almost any normal human being he is at moments uncomfortable. Most
of us are not disposed to tolerate such discomfort
for long save in connection with some cause or
issue that seems important.

Before considering more important men, let
us pause for a moment for a word about Anthony
Comstock, who came out of New England to
improve the morals of his countrymen and coun-
trywomen. He gave his life to a crusade against
vice, as described and perceived by him, and
against obscenity in particular. He was a brave
man, heroic in his labors, and incorruptible, but
even if he had not been so monstrous as to rejoice
in having driven fifteen people to suicide by his
exposures of personal vice, he would have been
a fit subject for caricature on other grounds. To

those who can view his activities in perspective he will ever appear as a petty figure because he attacked petty ills. One need not defend obscenity to regard him as a busybody and a common scold. Constant harping on trivial vices, even though they be generally recognized as vices, tends to make virtue itself seem priggish and unlovely, not as a positive good. Minor bastions can be mopped up in connection with larger movements against major obstacles; to the well-balanced mind they do not seem to deserve a lifelong campaign. History does not often pin medals on heroes of the trivial. Part at least of the measure of a reformer, the measure of his intelligence if not of his courage, is the evil that he attacks.

Of course reform may be constructive as well as destructive; the remedy may be emphasized as well as the disease. In moral and social therapeutics a surgical operation is generally insufficient. Failure to recognize the necessity of an adequate substitute for the evil that is attacked has not been an invariable characteristic of professional moral reformers, but unquestionably it has been a very common one. Doubtless they have thought of themselves as soldiers of the Lord in the warfare against sin, and have left to pastors and teachers the problem of bringing angels in to replace the devils that have been driven out. They have been indisposed to compromise with what they regard as sin, and when they have embarked upon social crusades have all too often limited themselves to "moral" questions, leaving the constructive tasks to politicians whom they have condemned as timeservers. Primarily, such men have been or have sought to be destroyers of evil. Their historic stature depends, accordingly, on posterity's judgment of the importance of the evils they sought to overthrow, of their effectiveness in combating them, and of the ultimate situation which resulted from their labors.

The most important reformers of this moral type who can be conveniently treated as a group are the Abolitionists, who crusaded against Negro slavery, and the Prohibitionists, who attacked the liquor traffic. The latter I can do little more than mention here, for the simple reason that sufficient biographical information about them is not yet available. Many of the limitations of the analogy between the two groups will be immediately apparent. Few will claim that the liquor traffic in itself was ever such an ill as the slave traffic, or that equal courage was required to combat it; but in individual Abolitionists and Prohibitionists the kinship of spirit was close, and, let me repeat, the emphasis here is not upon reform but upon reformers. In both cases, men of genuine religious spirit, along with some imposters, were engaged in what seemed to them a moral crusade against evil. Negro slavery is no longer a controversial subject, but all will agree that it was a major, not a minor, ill, and that the Abolitionists command attention at the bar of history.

In considering this important group let us begin with an extreme example, standing on the lunatic fringe of the movement. Let us begin with John Brown. At the time of his execution, following his famous raid at Harper's Ferry, he was regarded by many of the noblest spirits of his day as a major martyr to the cause of human freedom. In her diary Louisa M. Alcott recorded the execution of "Saint John the Just." Shortly before this, Emerson spoke of him publicly as "that new saint, than whom none purer or more brave was ever led by love of men into conflict and death, the new saint awaiting his martyrdom, and who, if he shall suffer, will make the gallows glorious like the cross." The Sage of Concord subsequently modified his judgment; and Abraham Lincoln, soon after the event, commented that, however worthy Brown's motives may have been, his action was futile and his philosophy was identical with that of any assassin, seeking to destroy one whom he regarded as a tyrant.[1]   In the light of present knowledge, the canonization of the Abolitionist martyr seems to have been premature.

It ought to have been evident, even then, that his emotions far outran his intelligence. Though a native of Connecticut, like so many of the Abolitionists, John Brown enjoyed few of the educational opportunities commonly associated with New England. Indeed, he grew up in Ohio, where he rejoiced more in the freedom of the wilderness than in the confinement of school. His background was one of distinct piety, but his intellect was narrow and untrained. Even more important is the fact that his mother, his mother's mother, and several other near relatives died insane. Affidavits about the man himself that were available at the time of his trial might have led a modern court to commit him to an asylum rather than to condemn him to the gallows.

Saddled with a large family, consistently unsuccessful in business, constantly on the move, he found an outlet for his moral zeal in the border warfare in Kansas. His unshakable conviction that he was the instrument of God cannot blind the eyes of any student to his deeds of unspeakable cruelty against innocent people.

---

[1] These and other contemporary comments can be conveniently seen in J. F. Rhodes, *History of the United States from the Compromise of 1850*, Vol. II (1900), pp. 410-14.

The motive power in his crusade was not love but hatred, and by none of the criteria which common sense would apply was John Brown a saint. It is fairer to the Abolitionists and to him to describe him as a madman.

Proceeding inward from the lunatic fringe, we come to one who has often been described, not as a madman perhaps, but as a fanatic. William Lloyd Garrison in his day was the best known, not to say the most notorious, of the Abolitionists. He deserves more extended treatment.

Garrison's life began in humble circumstances in Newburyport, Massachusetts. His father, an intemperate sea captain, deserted the family when Lloyd was a small child, and the boy grew up in poverty without any formal schooling to speak of. Like Benjamin Franklin, he found his occupation and acquired his education in a printing office, but the analogy goes no further. Throughout his life Franklin's will and emotions were illuminated and directed by an ever-widening intelligence: Garrison's intense emotions and powerful will drove him along a narrow groove, from which he never emerged. His calling was that of an editor; he set the type for his own editorials in the *Liberator*. His life was that of a crusader, primarily against slavery, but also, after that fight was won, for Prohibition and woman's suffrage, against prostitution, and so on. From his crusading activity he gained what livelihood and what fame he had, and a very considerable amount of persecution. Never was there a better example of a professional reformer. His identification of himself with his cause was complete. It now appears, however, that his identification of Abolitionism with himself was unwarranted and unfortunate. To many he has seemed the evil genius of the movement.

It is hardly necessary to prove that his diatribes against slavery, against slaveholders, and against all who would not join him in vituperation were unmeasured. The fame of the *Liberator*, it has been said, was not owing to its Northern supporters but to its Southern enemies.[2] As so often happens, hatred bred hatred.

From the point of view of his fellow Abolitionists, except his small band of personal admirers, a further objection to the firebrand Garrison was that, at last, he could co-operate with no one. So far as the attainment of his ends was concerned his means were ineffective. He was a publicist, not an organizer; and in the end he denounced all who would not accept his counsels of immoderation. The churches of the South, dependent on a slaveholding society and indisposed to break

[2] G. H. Barnes, *The Antislavery Impulse* (New York, Appleton-Century, 1933), p. 50.

with it, he regarded as beneath contempt. Even the orthodox churches of the North he termed "cages of unclean birds, Augean stables of pollution," while he described the clergy as a "Brotherhood of Thieves." Within little more than a decade from the launching of his crusade, he described the Constitution as "a covenant with death and an agreement with Hell," and on July 4, 1854, he publicly burned that document. Autocratic and self-righteous in his judgments, he was in philosophy little short of an anarchist. He was indifferent to labor conditions in the North and had no constructive program to offer to the South or to the republic. He simply denounced the institution of slavery with unmatched power of vituperation.

That Garrison can be described as a saint is exceedingly doubtful. At any rate, organized religion cannot be blamed for his aberrations. He was brought up as a Baptist, and from the point of view of personal morality remained closest to the Evangelicals. But, beginning to denounce all the churches as false to their mission, he ultimately attacked doctrines themselves. He ceased to have any connection with organized religious activity and came to be commonly regarded as an infidel.

That he was fed by inner springs of power is unquestionable. Thus did he become unconquerable. In this sense he was and remained religious, but by no stretch of the imagination can he be termed Christian. He stands as a classic example of fanaticism, which William James has defined as "loyalty carried to a convulsive extreme."[3] As James continues, "Fanaticism is found only where the character is masterful and aggressive." The fault lay, not in the weakness of the will, but in the narrowness of the intelligence.

In Garrison, as in many other reformers, there was cruelty of temper because of excess of devotion to a cause. To devotees of the same cause, no inconsistency may here appear. Almost anything is justified by fanatics in the name of a cause, whether this be German Nationalism, Communism, Abolitionism, or the overthrow of Demon Rum. Loyalty is carried to "a convulsive extreme." There is, for example, not the slightest respect for property rights; even a consideration of them seemed pusillanimous to a man like Garrison. Some foes of capitalism in our day have the same point of view. We now find different aims, different causes, but among some people at least a similar temper. Humor is generally conspicuous by its absence. The most important corrective is a broader intellectual conception. The cause to which one is loyal must

---

[3] *The Varieties of Religious Experience,* p. 340.

be conceived in a big, not a narrow way. God
must be thought of, not as a tribal deity, or merely
as the Lord of justice, but as a God of infinite
compassion, whose sun shines on the just and the
unjust. The loyal worshipers of such a God
perceive at last that evil can be overcome only by
good.

Oliver Wendell Holmes, the Autocrat of the
Breakfast Table, in the days of Abolition casti-
gated reformers in a poem entitled "The Moral
Bully." However, in the course of the Civil
War, in which his son was so bravely fighting,
he made a speech on the Fourth of July (1863)
in which he spoke more tolerantly. Reformers,
he said, "may be unwise, violent, abusive, extravagant, impracticable, but they are alive, at any
rate, and it is their business to remove abuses
as soon as they are dead, and often to help them
die."[4] His description of reformers as moral
scavengers is not wholly complimentary, but it
seems to me a little too complimentary for Garrison. Anyone who was dominated by hatred as
he was, and who did so much to breed unnecessary hatred in others, stands in history as a de-
stroyer of good as well as evil.

In other men, Abolitionism may be seen not
only in more religious, but also in more effective
form. The interpretation of the great sectional

---

[4] *Writings,* Riverside ed. (1895), Vol. VIII, p. 90.

conflict as a clearcut struggle between right and wrong was long ago discarded, and in recent years historians have generally disregarded religious factors and have emphasized the economic rather than the political. The antislavery crusade itself has been interpreted by many students as predominantly economic; and the war between the sections has been regarded as a duel between rival economic systems, which could not live together comfortably in a united republic. Of late, however, there has been among scholars a renewed emphasis on religious factors.[5] According to this later view, although political and economic factors may have been dominant in the end, the original impulse and the dynamic force were predominantly religious. Even if this thesis be not fully accepted, the religious character of the early antislavery leaders seems indisputable, and it is the leaders rather than the movement that we are considering here.

It appears, then, that the effective antislavery movement started with the religious revival of Charles G. Finney, which reached its climax in 1830, and was best personified in Theodore Dwight Weld, who was not a sensational publicist like Garrison but a self-effacing organizer, so self-effacing indeed that even now his name is

---

[5] Gilbert H. Barnes, *The Antislavery Impulse*, p. vii. I have leaned heavily on this important book.

little known.   It seems clear that if Garrison
was the evil genius of Abolitionism, Weld represents the cause at its purest and best.   Garrison
broke with organized religion and was regarded
as an infidel; Weld and his band worked through
the churches and were profoundly religious men.
James G. Birney, the "reformed" Southern
slaveholder who became the candidate of the
Liberty party for the Presidency of the United
States, described Weld as "the most simple
hearted and earnest follower of Christ" he had
ever known.[6]   In a real sense these men were
religious crusaders of reform, and many of them
were saints.

Before speaking of Weld who symbolized the
group, we should say something of Charles G.
Finney, under whom he was converted and who
was probably the greatest American evangelist
between Whitefield and Dwight L. Moody.   It
is worthy of note that he, like so many of the
antislavery leaders who were enkindled by him,
was born in Connecticut, grew up on New England's religious frontier in New York state, and
in later life was identified with the Middle West,
where effective Abolitionism was at its strongest.
He took a pronounced stand on the slavery question, but, as he said, did not make a hobby of it.
Primarily, he was an evangelist of personal reli-

_____
[6] Barnes, p. 70.

gion. Theologically, he represented and implemented the new and revolting Calvinism, which was as revivifying an influence in the Western churches as was the Unitarian revolt in literary and intellectual circles in New England, and which had as its fruitage not merely the quickening of personal religion but also a new emphasis on social reform.

After a decade of free-lance evangelistic work in the nearer West, Finney invaded New York City, where he had the financial backing of the Tappan brothers, the philanthropists who did so much to support the antislavery cause. The Broadway Tabernacle was built for him, and there he ceased to be a Presbyterian and became a Congregationalist. In 1835, supported by Arthur Tappan, he established the theological department of Oberlin College. With few interruptions he remained at this center of aggressive Abolitionism and social reform for the rest of his life, serving for fifteen years as president, though always remaining in spirit and practice an evangelist. He now appears as not only an extraordinarily dynamic personality, but also as a strikingly symbolical figure. In him the New England religious temperament, liberated by life on the frontier, shook off the shackles of theological rigidity and manifested itself in the spirit of social betterment.

Of the reformers whom he inspired, Theodore Dwight Weld was probably the greatest. Also born in Connecticut, Weld was the son of a Congregational minister and moved with his family to New York state, near Utica, in his boyhood. At Utica in 1825 he was converted under Finney. Joining Finney's "holy band" of evangelists, he preached for a number of months in western New York and subsequently, during vacations, worked for the cause of temperance. He was converted to Abolitionism by Captain Charles Stuart, a retired British army officer, who was for a time principal of Utica Academy and bore Weld's expenses during part of his schooling. In due course he met the philanthropists Arthur and Lewis Tappan of New York City, who were Finney's backers, and converted them to Abolitionism. They were New Englanders, devoted to good works, and without a trace of humor.

The story of Weld's life thereafter is essentially that of the effective Abolition movement, of which he was the heart and to a large extent the brains. Commissioned by the Tappans to find a site for a seminary where Finney's converts might be trained, he selected Lane Seminary in Cincinnati and supplied most of the students. Among them in 1834 he organized a debate on slavery, destined to become famous. Although the wrath of the trustees and of President Lyman

Beecher was aroused, young Henry Ward Beecher and his sister Harriet (Beecher Stowe) were won over completely.

Previous to this, Weld in the course of his travels had enlisted in the Abolitionist cause James G. Birney, whom he met in Alabama, and three members of the faculty of Western Reserve College, President Charles B. Storrs, Elizur Wright, and Beriah Green. Birney, a layman and lawyer, became in due course one of the most conspicuous advocates of political activity against slavery, in direct opposition to Garrison, and was twice the candidate of an antislavery party for President. The three professors of Western Reserve soon aroused local opposition in Ohio. Storrs shortly died but Wright and Green became noted Abolitionists. They too were born in Connecticut. Elizur Wright became an active official of the American Anti-Slavery Society, and in later life was a pioneer actuary, an advocate of reform in life insurance, and a champion of conservation. After leaving Western Reserve, Beriah Green, who was a Congregational clergyman, became president of Oneida Institute, Whitesboro, New York, which Weld had attended; and afterward, for a decade or more, was pastor of a local church which had been formed by seceding Abolitionists.

If the influence of Weld in gaining these im-

portant recruits may seem to have been exaggerated, there can be no denying the essential unity
of the group. Even more effective service may
have been rendered by him in training the young
Abolitionists who were expelled from Lane Seminary and many of whom transferred to Oberlin.
At this time the American Anti-Slavery Society
was suffering unpopularity and embarrassment
because of its advocacy of immediate emancipation, which sounded too much like Garrison.
Their qualification of this motto by the statement that immediate emancipation was to be
gradually accomplished seemed contradictory
and required a vast amount of explanation.

At this juncture Weld trained a group of
Lane Rebels and sent them forth as agents of
the society, to win converts to Abolitionism. As
they went from town to town, they did not emulate William Lloyd Garrison's fiery and sensational journalism: they employed Finney's
methods of personal evangelism. It appears that
the regions that were evangelized by them became the chief seats of antislavery strength in
later years. Chief among the agents, next to
Weld himself, was Henry B. Stanton, another
native of Connecticut who removed to New York
state and was there converted by Finney. He
was regarded by many people as the best antislavery orator of the day, and has another title to

fame in that he was the husband of Elizabeth Cady Stanton. After a few years the American Anti-Slavery Society, finding evangelism more effective than pamphlet warfare, enlarged the missionary band to seventy. Weld selected and trained the recruits. Among them was a Southern Quaker, Angelina Grimké, whom he afterward married.

Into the last phases of Weld's extraordinary crusade, when he was a power behind the legislative scenes in Washington, supplying ammunition to John Quincy Adams and others, we shall not enter here because our chief concern is with the more religious phases of the movement. It might be pointed out that *Uncle Tom's Cabin* was based in part at least on his tract, *American Slavery As It Is*, but chief emphasis here must be laid on his evangelism, whereby he gave to his cause a definite religious sanction. His influence, through his converts and the many statesmen whom he influenced, entitles him to recognition as the greatest of all the Abolitionists.

Fame would have been accorded him sooner had he been less modest. Publicity such as Garrison rejoiced in was viewed by Weld with horror. He would accept no office, even in an antislavery society, and would speak at no convention; his tracts were published without his name; and his labors in town and country were unreported. But the man who was described by Lyman Beecher as "logic on fire" and by Elizabeth Whittier as an archangel, was of large and heroic mold. To him personal honor was less than nothing: the cause was everything. Moral reform can have no purer symbol.

The character and motives of such a man withstand almost any test that human judgment can apply. Nonetheless, the cause in which he submerged his personality and the methods which he and his converts used must be subjected to critical analysis. Upon its surface, Abolitionism of this brand seems less censorious and much more reasonable than that of William Lloyd Garrison, though the difference between the two schools appears to have been one of methods rather than objectives. The tactics of the Weld group were incomparably superior and infinitely more successful. Garrison was a reckless pamphleteer; Weld, with all his intelligence, was an evangelist of reform, seeking to win hearts and kindle emotions. Beyond a doubt he chose the better way.

It may seem ungenerous to say of a man so wise and good that he was at best a moral critic and not a builder. Like so many evangelists, he emphasized the sin that was to be eradicated, not the goodness that was to be enthroned. Indeed, there is deep significance in the fact that the best of the religious Abolitionists designated

slavery as a moral sin rather than as a social evil.
Living in a region which, by fortunate accidents
of climate and history, was spared the dread problems of slavery, they addressed themselves primarily to nonslaveholders and convinced them
of the iniquity of human bondage. They fired
inhabitants of free states with zeal to extirpate
sin from the lives of others, who were far removed and lived under very different conditions.
They assumed the task of rebuke, leaving to
others the painful task of social reconstruction.

It is not surprising that men who were born
without their consent into a society of which slavery was a part saw in this attitude uncharitable
self-righteousness. Perception of an evil is indeed the first step in all reform, but statesmanship requires the recommendation of a feasible,
or at least a possible remedy. Denunciation is
not enough. Agitation that begins among the
beneficiaries of an evil, or among those who are
innocently enmeshed in it, is so heroic that it
borders on the superhuman, and it may be that
the impulse to reform must generally be started
from without; but the whole history of the effort
to correct the wrong of slavery was marked by
a lack of realism that now seems incredible. In
the process other wrongs were inflicted, which
the reformers did not foresee or of which they
were oblivious. It is this sort of blind spot in

reformers that explains the dislike which men of common sense so often have for them. The historian must recognize that times often come when society needs to be shocked from its indolence and complacency; but the common man is likely to continue to believe that a society composed primarily of reformers would be an exceedingly unpleasant one to live in.

Indeed, if we confine ourselves to the hundred-per-cent Abolitionists, and eliminate the literary group, who were unquestionably quickened by them but were rarely willing to go with them all the way, it may be claimed that few movements of comparable influence have produced so few appealing personalities. The reason can be set forth in the moral that Hawthorne draws in *The Blithedale Romance* on the character of Hollingsworth, whom he terms a professional philanthropist, but whom we should call a reformer. Admitting that professional philanthropy is "often useful by its energetic impulse to society at large, it is perilous to the individual whose ruling passion, in one exclusive channel, it thus becomes. It ruins, or is fearfully apt to ruin, the heart, the rich juices of which God never meant should be pressed violently out, . . . by an unnatural process, but should render life sweet, bland, and gently beneficent, and insensibly influence other lives and other hearts to the same blessed end."[7] This romanticist may be preaching a counsel of perfection, but it does seem true that the reformer, who may and often does purify society as by fire, rarely wins the hearts of his fellow creatures and sometimes loses his own.

The Abolitionists were hard, as men of moral temper so often are; they were fighters, not seers or poets; their compassion toward helpless slaves often expressed itself in cruelty to hapless masters, and to the social order in which the despised institution was enmeshed; they were not historically or scientifically minded, and overlooked embarrassing economic analogies with forms of Northern industrial slavery; in general, their courage and zeal were greater than their intelligence or humanity. The war itself was a result of complex forces, but for long years it seemed that the cure of slavery was almost worse than the disease.

In view of our present knowledge of social therapeutics (whatever may be said of our practice), the methods advocated by the Abolitionists seem almost as crude as the surgery that was employed, without anaesthetics, before the Civil War. However, we can no more judge these reformers than we can early practioners of medicine on the basis of the knowledge which our own

[7] *Works* (1883), Vol. V, p. 593.

generation possesses. The analogy is imperfect because society has advanced farther in surgery and medicine than in the cure of social ills, but at least it suggests that no fair judgment can be passed on any individual without regard to the times in which he lived.

It must be recognized that the Abolitionists as a group represented one of the chief moral forces of their generation, and that if the cure of an evil brought other evils in its train, this is a lesson in methods, not ethics. They overemphasized existing wrong; for a generation historians have been toning down their overdrawn picture. Nonetheless, there was a great wrong, as many people in recent years seem to have forgotten. The major error of the Abolitionists, as of many other reformers, was in their oversimplification of a fearfully complex problem and in their indiscriminate attack on alleged wrongdoers rather than on wrong itself. Yet they were men of heroic mold and only a callous generation can be blind to their moral worth. To have muzzled them would have been to invite decay.

No millennium followed the appeal to arms. The road to human freedom was longer than they thought, and man's inhumanity to man appeared immediately in other forms after the legality of one sort of slavery disappeared. After all, the front on which they fought was too narrow. But at their best they fought a brave fight, and their heroic spirit, enlightened by a higher intelligence and tempered by a more Christian charity, could well be used today. The need for fighting saints may be perennial; but never in our time has it been so great as now.

IV

SOME WOMEN SAINTS

SINCE fiery John Knox sounded "The first Blast of the Trumpet against the Monstrous Regiment of Women," chief among them his enemy, Mary Queen of Scots, the feminine contingent in the Christian army has grown steadily in size and in recognition until no one would now dream of questioning its importance. Indeed, the most extreme antifeminists of the last two generations loudly asserted that, next after the home, the place of women was in the church and the school. To this there has been agreement even in Germany.

Even in our own land of "emancipated" women, however, they have rarely been high officials in the organized church. Among them can be numbered at least one religious founder, who is regarded by many people as the most important woman in the recorded history of America. I have no thought of minimizing the significance of Mrs. Mary Baker Eddy, first saint of Christian Science, but I have troubles enough already without embarking upon a discussion of her highly controversial career. If we confine ourselves to more conventional religious groups,

84

we may find in their failure to grant official or
clerical status to women an evidence that the
organized church as an institution is much more
conservative than organized education or the
state itself. After strenuous exertions over a
period of years, Dr. Anna Howard Shaw became
a fully recognized minister of the Methodist
Protestant Church, but ordination has generally
been restricted to the dominant males. The wisdom or unwisdom of this policy I am not dis-
cussing here. Some may say that even without
women ministers the Church is overfeminized
already. The point is, merely, that one must
look elsewhere than on the rolls of the clergy or
of ecclesiastical officials for distinguished American women who may be designated as saintly.

It need hardly be said that in our historic past
the fields of achievement open to women have
been sharply restricted, and that, in comparison
with men, the number of them who have gained
distinction has been small. In this connection, I
made a survey of all the women included in the
twenty volumes of the *Dictionary of American
Biography* and found that there were slightly
more than six hundred of them. They comprise
less than five per cent of the whole, fewer than
one in twenty. If we were considering our own
generation alone, of course, the percentage would

be considerably higher, but even now it would be relatively small.

In stating this well-known fact my last thought is to reflect upon the women. Jane Addams once quoted the French proverb: "Men make the roads, but it is women who teach children how to walk."[1] Theirs may be regarded as the more important task, and certainly it is the more human, but it does not bring a commensurate reward in publicity or prominence. The building of a new highway may be described in the newspapers; but the teaching of a little child to walk is unlikely to be recorded anywhere except in a mother's diary. Any chronological survey of distinguished American women will reveal their marked increase in number with the passing years, but in bygone times the noblest and saintliest among them may have been known to only a restricted circle.

A further analysis of these six hundred names reveals interesting information about their distribution among occupations. More than one third of them gained their fame chiefly as writers. At first glance this percentage seems astounding. Even among men it is true that writers, like politicians, gain and have long gained disproportionate and somewhat artificial prominence. As sub-

---

[1] *The Second Twenty Years at Hull House* (New York, The Macmillan Company, 1930), p. 99.

jects of historical investigation, writers have at
least left a record, and they may well have assumed historical importance greater than they
deserve. Nonetheless, it was a great boon to an
aspiring woman, forbidden or unable to don the
sword or to ascend pulpit or rostrum, that she
could take up the pen.

Few professions or avocations are so compatible
with domesticity as the literary calling. Elizabeth Stuart Phelps, speaking of her mother, for
whom she was named and who was also a writer,
said that her last book and her last baby came
together and killed her. At that time many men
doubtless blamed the book, and nowadays some
women might blame the baby; but it is generally
recognized that the two may go together and that
consequences need not be disastrous. Said Elizabeth Stuart Phelps the daughter: "She lived one
of those rich and piteous lives such as only gifted
women know; torn by the civil war of the dual
nature which can be given to women only. It
was as natural for her daughter to write as to
breathe; but it was impossible for her daughter
to forget that a woman of intellectual power
could be the most successful of mothers."[2] In
any case the reconciliation between genius and
domestic life may be difficult, but the daughter
who always understood that her mother must

[2] Elizabeth Stuart Phelps, *Chapters From a Life* (1896), p. 12.

write books, could not remember a time when her children needed her and did not find her.

In her recent autobiography, Edna Ferber, speaking of the Jews, says that "again and again deprived of property, of liberty, of land, of human rights, we have turned to the one thing of which only death can rob us: creative self-expression."[3] She might have used the same words about gifted women in the past, for they have known how to turn their sorrow as well as their joy into song.   Despite the fact that so many other means of self-expression are now open to women, it seems probable that nowhere else do they compete with men on such terms of equality as in literature.   The profession of letters in this country enjoys slight security but a maximum of freedom; restrictions and limitations based on race, geography, or sex hardly exist at all.   It need surprise no one, therefore, if on any list of the most noted American women of our own time a goodly number of writers should appear.

Among the six hundred distinguished women of the past, whom we mentioned just now, educators come next to writers though they are much less numerous.   The two other major classes consist of reformers and actresses.   Considering the number of women teachers and the growing

---

[3] Edna Ferber, *A Peculiar Treasure* (New York, Doubleday, Doran, 1939), p. 60.

emphasis during the past two generations on the higher education of women, one need not be surprised at the proportions of the educational group. Prominence in this field, however, is considerably dependent upon official position and, though schools are less conservative in this respect than churches, the higher places are still likely to go to men. The activities of women in reform have gone along with and have been a natural outgrowth of literary effort. Any number of noted writers, like Harriet Beecher Stowe, may also be described as reformers; and almost all the feminine reformers have had recourse to the written word. Access to the public rostrum came later, as a rule, though Susan B. Anthony and Frances E. Willard became more noted for their speeches than their books.

Of the theatrical group we need say little here. It has long been obvious that if the drama is to depict human life both sexes must be represented in it. Accordingly, women were winning fame upon the stage before they dared ascend the lecture platform to advocate any of the causes dearest to their hearts. This avenue of distinction is still wide open to women, and as Charlotte Cushman appears on lists of notables drawn from the more distant past, Mrs. Minnie Maddern Fiske appears on those drawn from our own decade. The dramatic instinct, though present in many

great preachers like George Whitefield, is not
generally regarded as an accompaniment of the
religious spirit.   With the actresses, then, we
shall not concern ourselves further than to pay
them passing tribute.   Rather shall we devote
attention to women who, though relatively un-
welcome in the official circles of churches, have
expressed the religious impulse in literature and
even more notably in reform, education, and
humanitarianism.

Of the writers, I want to speak briefly of three:
Elizabeth Stuart Phelps, Harriet Beecher Stowe,
and Julia Ward Howe.   Miss Phelps, who later
became Mrs. Ward, we shall consider first because of the trio she was least a reformer.   This
product of the gentle beauty of Andover, in the
mellow autumn of New England theology, was
essentially a comforter.

Elizabeth Stuart Phelps happened to be born
in Boston, though she was soon transferred to the
countryside and took root there.   Very modestly
she said that her literary abilities all belonged
to her ancestors.   She might have laid equal
stress on her religious inheritance.   Her mother,
whose promising literary career was cut short by
early death, was the daughter of Moses Stuart,
professor of sacred literature at Andover Theological Seminary for a long generation.   A notable Hebraist and conservative theologian, he

was enormously influential as a teacher of clergymen. Calvin E. Stowe, husband of Harriet
Beecher, was one of his pupils, and for a time in
later years was a professor in the Seminary. Her
father, Austin Phelps, who provided her climate,
she said, and was in some way the hero of every
chapter in her life, became professor of sacred
literature and homiletics at Andover the year
that Moses Stuart died, and remained there for
more than three decades.

From such a background of theology and piety
this woman novelist emerged. She published
stories and a number of Sunday-school books.
Then, in the sadness of the years after the Civil
War, when so many women were mourning their
husbands and their sons, she wrote, during two
years in an unheated room, her most successful
book, *Gates Ajar*. Into a "great world of woe,"
she said, "my little book stole forth, trembling."
She said that the writing of it was so inevitable
that she felt she had no more to do with it than
the bough through which the wind cries. "The
angel said unto me 'Write!' and I wrote."[4] She
hoped it would bring some comfort and, though
a later generation would regard it as excessively
Biblical, this story of a heaven of light and love
accomplished its purpose.

Among her many other books we shall men-

---

[4] *Chapters From a Life,* p. 95.

tion only one, written almost a generation later, after she had come to know and sympathize with the hard-bitten, hard-drinking fishermen of Gloucester. The story of the Christlike minister which she tells in *A Singular Life* reflects the final emphasis of this daughter and granddaughter of theologians. To a sophisticated and aimless generation novels written with an ethical purpose may seem less than art, but as she said: "Our book reveals what life is to us. Life is to us what we are."[5] To others I will leave the technical judgments and will merely say that here is gentle saintliness expressing itself in literary form.

The story of Harriet Beecher Stowe, whom Elizabeth Stuart Phelps knew at Andover, and described as the greatest of American women, is too well known to require retelling, but I cannot forbear remarking on her background. She was born at Litchfield, Connecticut, the daughter of Lyman Beecher, an eminent clergyman who was more conservative on the slavery question than the two most distinguished of his many distinguished children. The son and grandson of blacksmiths, this robust man had three wives and thirteen sons and daughters, six of whom, including Henry Ward Beecher, were clergymen. Besides Harriet, another daughter, Cath-

---

[5] *Chapters From a Life,* p. 260.

erine, attained considerable prominence as an
educator and reformer. An extraordinary family, by any standard! Harriet was next in age
and closest in spirit to Henry.

Her education was overwhelmingly religious,
and, after much doubt and conflict, she was "converted" at fourteen. The conflict between faith
and doubt runs through all her writings. In Cincinnati, where her father was the head of Lane
Seminary, she married Calvin E. Stowe, a minister, scholar, and pioneer advocate of public education. If she hadn't had so many children
(seven altogether) she might have started writing sooner. In Cincinnati, as was pointed out in
an earlier lecture, she was greatly affected by
the Abolitionist sentiment inspired by Theodore
D. Weld, but not until she went to Brunswick,
Maine, where her wandering husband became
professor at Bowdoin, did she write *Uncle Tom's
Cabin*, the most famous best-seller of antebellum
times and the most important literary factor in
the spread of antislavery sentiments. It was
probably more influential than all the sober antislavery tracts of the era put together.

There is no need at this late date to describe
or discuss what is in some respects the most
famous of American novels. As a Southerner
who did not read it until after he was grown
may I say, however, that it proved to be a far

more sympathetic treatment than I had antici-
pated. Its author I should expect to be, as
biographical studies show that she was, far more
warm-hearted than the great body of the Abolitionists. No mere moralist but a born story-
teller, she worked in a richer medium. She stands
as an example of the Puritan spirit, inveterate in
its reforming tendencies, but liberated and hu-
manized in the West, and with a distinctive fire
and warmth that was inborn. There was about
her an endearing lack of practicality and a certain
rich luxuriance. As a saint she was, like her
famous brother, robust and hearty.

Julia Ward Howe came of an even more distinguished family. She was born in New York
City, the daughter of Samuel Ward, a rich
banker who could trace his paternal line back
through an unbroken line of distinguished men to
a colonial governor of Rhode Island. Her husband, Samuel Gridley Howe, won an honored
place in history for his services to the blind, the
deaf, the insane, the imprisoned, to the causes of
public education and antislavery. It is not surprising that this pair had remarkably distinguished children who married well. The record
of this family, from colonial times to the present,
has been rarely if ever equaled in American history.

Her marriage to a man eighteen years her

senior and noted for his benevolence revealed
the native seriousness of a woman born to wealth
and opportunity. She traveled widely and had distinguished friends everywhere, was a student of
philosophy and language, wrote travel sketches
and poetry. Relatively late in the antislavery
movement she became active in it, and, during
the Civil War, after a visit to a camp near Washington, she wrote the "Battle Hymn of the Republic." After the war she was actively interested in all causes affecting women and was the
president of many organizations. Despite her
generous support of worthy movements, hers was
not the life or the temper of the full-time reformer; her interests were too broad and her
personality too well-rounded for that. Despite
the sincerity of her progressive democracy, she
was in the best sense an aristocrat and lived in
splendid isolation. In religious connection a
Unitarian, she occasionally preached sermons, but
this very distinguished lady would doubtless be
surprised to find herself in a gallery of saints.

The most notable women of her generation
who were in a stricter sense reformers, and some
of whom must be termed professionals because
they devoted themselves completely to reform,
comprised a close-knit group, banded in a common cause. The Cause was the rights of women,
especially suffrage, but associated with it and

overlapping it were temperance, higher education, and various humanitarian movements. The
oldest and greatest of the suffragists, Lucretia
Mott, Elizabeth Cady Stanton, and Susan B.
Anthony, began their careers as advocates of
other causes, chiefly antislavery and temperance,
and, finding themselves blocked by restrictions
imposed upon their sex, turned to woman's suffrage as the fundamental reform by which the
others would be furthered. Frances E. Willard,
who became the symbol of the W.C.T.U., was
also a suffragist; and Dr. Anna Howard Shaw divided her activities between the two causes until
Miss Anthony convinced her that it was wiser to
concentrate upon one. "You can't win two causes
at once," said Aunt Susan. "You're merely scat-
tering your energies. Begin at the beginning.
Win suffrage for women, and the rest will follow."[6]

This single-minded devotion was also exemplified, in the case of the wisest of these leaders,
by their personal repudiation of oddities which
might prove an obstacle. Thus Doctor Shaw
ceased wearing her hair short, and Susan B. Anthony abandoned the "bloomer" costume, which
for a time before the Civil War she had worn for
comfort and as a symbol of independence, but
which, as she soon found, distracted attention

---

[6] Anna Howard Shaw, *The Story of a Pioneer* (1915), p. 182.

from the words she spoke. She had learned the lesson, she said, "that to be successful a person must attempt but one reform." Advocacy of minor reforms, like customs of dress, may make one ridiculous, while the championing of a major cause may make one great. The movement for the rights of women, which affected half the population of the country, if not half the human race, was unquestionably important, and among its American leaders were some truly great women.

The earliest of the major pioneers were Lucretia Mott and Elizabeth Cady Stanton, who launched the movement for woman's suffrage at the first woman's rights convention at Seneca Falls, New York, in 1848. Mrs. Mott, whose career centered in Philadelphia, was born on Nantucket of Quaker stock and was an "acknowledged minister" of the Society of Friends, though she managed to bring up five children. Her chief activities were in the early and relatively unfruitful years of the woman's movement, and were more largely devoted to antislavery than to feminism. Of her spiritual quality and her reforming zeal there has been and can be no question.

Mrs. Stanton was born in upstate New York and grew up in a stern religious atmosphere of the Presbyterian sort. She also began her reforming career in the antislavery cause, but, being

more than a score of years younger than Lucretia
Mott, she lived long enough to collaborate with
Susan B. Anthony and to share honors with her
during a generation that was more fruitful in the
woman's movement. She was also touched by its
educational current, being a graduate of Emma
Willard's famous seminary at Troy, New York.
She married the noted Abolitionist orator, Henry
Brewster Stanton, and bore him seven children,
all told. In the course of her long life she often
lectured on the bringing up of a family, as well as
upon woman's suffrage. Until her death in 1902
she worked in the closest co-operation with Susan
B. Anthony. Of the two she was the more brilliant conversationalist and the more ready
speaker, but for family reasons, if for no other,
she was unable to devote herself so completely
to the Cause. On one occasion Miss Anthony,
who was generally more accurate than she in
regard to exact facts and dates, had questioned a
statement of hers in regard to the time at which
a particular incident had occurred. Mrs. Stanton
clinched the matter by saying, "I tell you it happened when I was weaning Harriet. What event
have you got to reckon from?"[7] This flabber-
gasted the spinster who had had no similar experience. These two matrons, Mrs. Mott and
Mrs. Stanton, and the old maid, Miss Anthony,

---

[7] Shaw, *Story of a Pioneer*, p. 242.

form the trinity of American feminism. By their collaborators and most of womankind they were regarded as saints.

Susan B. Anthony may have been more single-minded because she remained single. The Cause was her love and the object of more than half a century of wholehearted devotion. She was born in Adams, Massachusetts, of Quaker stock. Her father was a cotton manufacturer of great moral courage and independence and she had an aunt who was a Quaker preacher. She taught school for a time but, with her active and aggressive nature, found the schoolroom confining. In moral standards she was severe and, during her young womanhood at least, rather priggish. In later years, when she found an outlet for her abundant energies in lecture tours, campaigns, and conventions, she grew more tolerant and mellow. This dauntless crusader even voted, illegally, upon one occasion at least and refused to pay the fine that was imposed upon her. She was willing to ignore all law, she said, to free womankind from slavery.

In spirit she was nearer the Abolitionists than the humanitarians, though she was not devoid of humor. Honor came to her in the end, but she did not seek it; the Cause was everything. In striving for its triumph, she did not heed trifles like heat, cold, hunger, or fatigue. She was

known to talk all night about the Cause and then
to rush off to a committee meeting and a public
session, reluctantly conceding that it might be
well to drink a cup of coffee. Her last public
words were "Failure is impossible." In spirit
she was a pioneer woman and, not inappropriately, success first came to her cause in the West,
where she campaigned so often and so arduously.
That she was fed by inner fires and deserves the
hero's reward is unquestionable.

She told Anna Howard Shaw that the people
in the West didn't seem to know much about
Quakers and wouldn't admit that she was religious. So she wanted the public support of a
Methodist. Doctor Shaw, whom she proudly
introduced as an ordained Methodist minister,
did give her support in many a campaign, and
was one of the most effective lieutenants who
carried on the movement after the passing of
Aunt Susan. Anyone would have welcomed the
aid of this sturdy woman who spent her adoles-
cent years in the wilderness in Michigan, battled
her way through college, theological school, and
medical school, and even into the ranks of the
ordained clergy. Born in England, she came to
America when she was a little child, lived in
Lawrence, Massachusetts, until she was twelve,
and was then taken by her parents into the wilderness. Her parents were Unitarians, but she

gained encouragement and a preacher's license from the Methodists and henceforth associated herself with them.

During her struggling college days at Albion College, she fought for the rights of women students and lectured on temperance and filled pulpits whenever she got a chance. Her theological studies in Boston were pursued under conditions of direst poverty. For seven years she served as a pastor on Cape Cod, studying medicine in Boston on the side, and then became a lecturer for temperance and woman's suffrage. A lecturer she remained all the rest of her life and probably she was the best among all the American women. Her strenuous activities for woman's suffrage continued for a generation; the Distinguished Service Medal was awarded her for her services as chairman of the Women's Committee of the Council of National Defense during the World War; and her death came as the result of overexertions in a speaking tour with William H. Taft and A. Lawrence Lowell in behalf of the League of Nations. In few women, or men either for that matter, has the religious spirit expressed itself in more vigorous and effective action.

Without prejudice I think it can be said that these women pioneers of reform, and those who were most conspicuously associated with them,

were a more attractive group than the Abolitionists, from whom in a sense they emerged and to
whom they were in many respects akin. Part of
their appeal undoubtedly lay in the fact that they
were women; in some sense the maternal spirit
was manifested in them all. More important
still is the fact that they advocated a constructive
rather than a destructive reform. It is true that
they attacked a powerful vested interest, the exclusive privileges of men, but their purpose was
to increase human opportunities, not to diminish
them. By gaining recognition for the rights of
women they hoped, and were warranted in hoping, that human society would be enriched. The
injustices which fell to the lot of women they
resented, and of the righteousness of their cause
they were convinced; but the exercise of privileges by men was not regarded by them as sinful.
Deeply religious as the leading suffragists were,
they were dealing, not with details of personal
morality, but with matters of broad social concern. The salient which they attacked was a vital
part of the larger front which democracy itself
was assailing. As Miss Anthony said, failure was
impossible unless democracy itself should fail.
It may be expected, therefore, that the fruits of
victory gained by these magnificent pioneers will
endure as long as republican institutions shall
survive.

We have already pointed out that the suffragists as a group were advocates of temperance, naturally enough in view of their concern for the well-being of children and the home. As the cause of woman's rights was marred by such absurdities as those associated with the names of Mrs. Amelia Jenks Bloomer and Dr. Mary Walker, who advocated dress reform prematurely, little dreaming that the time would come when women would feel free to discard practically all their clothing, so the temperance cause has had its freaks and oddities. The most notorious of these was Carry Nation, who was certainly not a great woman except in size and who gives no impression of saintliness. A reference to her is inserted by way of contrast. She might be described as the John Brown of the Prohibition movement, though she was essentially a comic rather than a tragic figure. The analogy is striking in this respect at least: her mother, her brother, and her sister were insane. She was like him also in that she was very ignorant. Since her first husband and only love was such a sot that he died of alcoholism after she had been forced to leave him, it is no wonder that she hated saloons. However, when she smashed them with her mighty hatchet this violent woman must have been mad. She may have served a purpose in dramatizing public hostility to the saloon, but she cannot be placed among the saints of temperance. She belongs on the extreme edge of the lunatic fringe.

The major feminine saint of temperance, of course, is Frances E. Willard. She was born in New York state of New England stock, her parents having come from Vermont. Both of them were teachers and they moved on to Oberlin, where they went to college; then they proceeded to the wilds of Wisconsin, where Frances grew up, largely out of doors. In after years she was admiringly decribed as "America's Uncrowned Queen," but her close friends called her "Frank." She attended Northwestern Female College, at Evanston, Illinois, was there "converted," and joined the Methodists. Entering temperance work at thirty-five, after a few years of teaching, she remained in it the rest of her life. In temperament, in vigor, and in tireless devotion she was much like the leading suffragists, with whom she co-operated closely and by whom she was fully appreciated. Like them she lectured all over the country, organized campaigns, conducted conventions, and devoted herself unstintedly to a movement. More than suffrage, however, hers was interpreted as a moral cause. She was not a narrow woman but her battle was fought, as perhaps it had to be at that time, on a relatively narrow front, not in the broader field of social relationships. This moral approach, which was characteristic of Miss Willard, increased the probabilities of immediate success among the churchly groups but may have served in the end to limit the appeal of temperance by defining it too sharply. The humanitarians who lived within the slums were no more sincere and self-sacrificing than the crusaders for personal purity, but they understood human nature better and perceived social conditions more clearly. They were no braver, but they fought on a broader front.

The humanitarians, however, I will leave till the last. Meanwhile, I want to say at least a passing word about the women educators, whose work was so constructive. Like the suffragists, they sought to extend to women privileges already enjoyed by men and thus to enrich human society. The first woman to take a conspicuous public stand for the higher education of her sex and to make definite experiments in that direction was Emma Hart Willard, who established the Troy Female Seminary in 1821. She antedated the suffragists and trained some of them, though her major influence was exerted through the education of teachers. She was a queenly woman, without the angularity associated with professional reformers, and she was dominated by ideals of human service. Born in Connecticut, she was one of the many great women contributed by New England.

Another was Mary Lyon, a native of Massachusetts and the founder of Mount Holyoke, which embodied her conviction that there should be an institution for women of similar permanence and curriculum with the colleges for men. With her also there was major emphasis on education as training for service.

As a third person in this Trinity of educational saints let us name Alice Freeman Palmer, who was born in New York state but is mostly identified in public memory with Wellesley and Cambridge. She was the daughter of a farmer, who later became a small-town physician, and she knew the hardships and joys of simple human life. Determined to have a college education as good as men could gain, she was admitted to the University of Michigan after much struggle, and a few years after her graduation was brought to Wellesley. She became acting president at the age of twenty-six and president the next year. Five years later she was married to Professor George Herbert Palmer. The romance of these two choice spirits has often been compared to that of Robert Browning and Elizabeth Barrett.

During her brief stay at Wellesley, Mrs. Palmer, then Miss Freeman, left the indelible impress of her personality upon it; she was for

the rest of her life an active member of its Board
of Trustees; and she rendered invaluable aid to
William Rainey Harper by serving, on a special
part-time arrangement, as Dean of Women of
the new University of Chicago. This frail but
extraordinarily active woman did innumerable
other services to a host of persons and causes, but
we cannot speak of them here. To few American women of her generation will saintliness be
more readily attributed. Throughout life she
was a devout Presbyterian, without cloud of
theological doubt and, as her husband said, all
her morality was "touched with a divine emotion."[8] As Richard Watson Gilder wrote, just
after her untimely death, "All her life was giving." The spiritual beauty of such a personality
can be better portrayed in verse like his than in
prose like mine.

Of the humanitarians we shall also mention
three. Clara Barton, founder of the American
Red Cross, stands apart from the others. Like
most of the other women whom we have considered she was born in New England, but although
she was brought up as a Universalist she was
never a member of a church. Distinctly an indi-
vidualist, she was regarded by many as arbitrary
and dictatorial, and was better qualified to initiate
a difficult undertaking than to carry it on in co-

---

[8] G. H. Palmer, *Alice Freeman Palmer* (1908), p. 346.

operation with others. Essentially practical, with great driving force, she was in no strict sense a reformer but she was profoundly devoted to human welfare.

Dorothea L. Dix, who was born in Maine and went to Boston when she was ten, has indisputable claims to saintliness. A Unitarian and member of the congregation of William Ellery Channing, she taught and traveled with his children and was deeply inspired by him to human service. This frail and gentle woman, first in Massachusetts and then in other states, investigated and disclosed the conditions to which insane persons were subjected; and in part as a result of her tireless efforts hospitals for the insane were established throughout the United States and a new era in the treatment of their unfortunate inmates was begun. Too timid to speak in public, she was exhaustless in her compassion.

This brings us to the last but by no means the least name on this roster, that of Jane Addams. During the final years of her life a number of lists of the greatest American women were issued under various auspices. On one of these, made after a poll of the National Council of Women for portraits for the Hall of Science at the Century of Progress Exposition in Chicago, she was ranked second among American women of all time; and on all the lists of women then living that I have seen she was ranked first. Following her death in 1935, the City Council of Chicago, on motion of the Mayor, adopted a resolution in which she was described as "the greatest woman who ever lived"; and other comments at the time were couched in language of even greater adulation. Without entering into the question of her relative distinction, we can say that probably no American woman has ever been canonized so quickly and by such an overwhelming voice.

Of all the women whom we have considered here, she was the only one born in the Middle West. The others almost without exception were natives of New England or its frontier in New York state. She was born in Cedarville, Illinois, whither her parents had come from Pennsylvania. Her father was a man of local prominence in business and politics and rejoiced in the friendship of Lincoln. It was said that there were other legislators in Illinois during the Civil War and Reconstruction who declined bribes, but that John H. Addams was the only legislator to whom nobody had dared to offer one. By tradition he was a Quaker and by practice a man of prayer, but his only creed was integrity and self-respect. He was not a communicant of any of the four local churches, but he was a generous contributor to all of them. No single individual influenced Jane Addams as much as her father.

She went to Rockford College, conducted by the redoubtable Miss Anna P. Sill, a remarkable woman whose chief ambition was to train Christian missionaries. To her the most famous graduate of the college has paid moving tribute, but in college she was something of a rebel against her. Jane was not a church member and had not even been baptized. One objection to Miss Sill she recorded in her notebook: "She does everything from love of God *alone*, and I do not like that."[9] Strong efforts were made to reach the small number of "unconverted" girls, but she says that she was "singularly unresponsive" to all forms of emotional appeal. She was destined to become a missionary of a very different sort. She gained some realization of the "beauty of holiness" during the Sunday morning hour when she read regularly with the Greek teacher from the Greek New Testament. At these sessions there was no syntax or doctrine.

Speaking of the years between her graduation and the establishment of Hull House, she afterward said: "During most of that time I was absolutely at sea as far as any moral purpose was concerned, clinging only to the desire to live in

[9] J. W. Linn, *Jane Addams* (New York, D. Appleton-Century Co., 1935), p. 44.

a really living world and refusing to be content with a shadowy intellectual or aesthetic reflection of it."[10] In this period, however, at the age of twenty-five, she received the rite of baptism and became a member of the Presbyterian church in Cedarville. She says that she was conscious of no emotional "conversion" and of no change from her childish acceptance of the teachings of the Gospels, but that something made her long for "an outward symbol of fellowship." Also, there was growing within her "an almost passionate devotion" to democratic ideals. "Who was I, with my dreams of universal fellowship, that I did not identify myself with the institutional statement of this belief, as it stood in the little village in which I was born, and without which testimony in each remote hamlet of Christendom it would be so easy for the world to slip back into the doctrines of selection and aristocracy?"[11]

Denominational connection never meant much to her. In later years she connected herself with a struggling little Congregational church around the corner from Hull House because it was convenient and needed her; but she ceased attendance during one period when she did not like the minister and was temporarily dropped from the rolls. During the months she spent in Europe,

[10] *Twenty Years at Hull House,* p. 64.
[11] *Ibid.,* pp. 77-79.

before coming to Chicago, she had gained the conception of a Settlement that "should unite in the fellowship of the deed those of widely differing religious beliefs."[12]

It was because of this fellowship which she inspired, this fellowship which knew no sect or race or class because it comprehended them all, that she was beloved by her coworkers and the immigrant matrons and the toughs and gamins of the city streets. To her the Settlement was infinitely more than a means to aid the destitute; it was also a means whereby those who were cut off by supposed good fortune from "the starvation struggle which makes up the life of at least half the race" were permitted to share that life and be vitalized by it. "To shut oneself away from that half of the race life," she said, "is to shut oneself away from the most vital part of it; it is to live out but half the humanity to which we have been born heir and to use but half our faculties."[13]

Whether or not the Settlement was or ever will be as effective an agency as she hoped, the necessity of bridging the gap between classes, nations, and racial groups for the benefit of the human race as a whole is even more plainly evident now than it was a generation ago. To the

[12] *Twenty Years at Hull House*, p. 83.
[13] *Ibid.*, pp. 116-17.

clashing factions of mankind this great advocate
of peace could say what she once said about a
Settlement: "There must be the overmastering
belief that all that is noblest in life is common
to men as men."[14] The thought is not new now,
and was not new then, but sincere and intelligent
exemplification of it is as rare as it is difficult.
This noble woman, whom her contemporaries did
not hesitate to describe as Christlike, was not primarily concerned with trivialities of personal
morality or taste, or even with the rights of
women as women, though they comprise half the
race, but with the universals of humanity itself.

[14] *Twenty Years at Hull House,* p. 124.

V

EVANGELISTS OF EDUCATION

FOR a much longer time than any of us can
remember, belief in universal education has
been a fundamental tenet in our democratic faith.
There have been innumerable controversies
about ways and means, but it has come to be regarded as a self-evident truth that every American child has the right to go to school, and that
the State is obligated to provide him with the
opportunity. How far educational opportunity
should extend is, and always will be, a matter of
opinion, but, until war, depression, and world-
wide fear caused the democratic ideal itself to
be challenged, the general American assumption
was that the sky was the limit. Educational opportunity, we have thought, should be as great
as can possibly be afforded, and each individual
should have a chance to make of himself all that
he can become. The sky seems much further off
than it used to, so this isn't a good time to talk
of limitless opportunity; but never has there been
a time when it was more important to reaffirm
our traditional faith in the power of enlightenment.

My purpose here, however, is not to argue for

a cause. It is to interpret the movement for universal education in America, or, rather, the careers of certain leaders of that movement, in terms of the religious spirit. In a real sense this has been a lay, not a clerical, movement, though many clergymen have been engaged in it. Popular education has been thought of, and properly thought of, as a corollary of political democracy; and the State has been recognized as the only agency that is strong enough to perform the gigantic task of training all the children of a huge country. Often in the past, efforts to extend the domain of public education have met with the open or covert opposition of organized religious groups. Fortunately for our domestic peace, in this land of multifarious religious sects, it has not been generally believed that education, even at its lower levels, is an exclusive state function. Into the question of the legitimate part which may be played by the Catholic Church or the Methodist Church or any other church in the formal processes of education we need not enter here. Suffice it to say that the increasing recognition of the necessary agency of the State or some one of its subdivisions has carried with it an increasing lay emphasis; and that, in times past if not now, this has caused many devout people to think of the crusade for popular education as

nonreligious at its best, and irreligious at its
worst.

Much depends, of course, on how one defines
"religious." The definition of "saint" which we
have adopted here is sufficiently broad to cover
most of the leaders of this crusade whose careers
I have surveyed. Though generally nonsectarian in emphasis, they were men and women of
sacrificial zeal and heroic labors, and they were
fed by inner springs of spiritual power. To them
the cause of education was a sort of religion, and
a very vital sort. In my own very churchly youth
I heard the venerable head of a Southern state
university say, in sentimental but very impressive
language, that if the Lord Jesus were to return
to earth in our time, he would find a large number of His disciples among humble teachers in the
public schools. Among the leaders of the historic crusade for public education in this country,
I am sure that many can be found who deserve
to be termed apostles. Some of them were as
true saints as ever breathed the air of earth.

The most famous apostle of public education
in America, in his or any other time, was Thomas
Jefferson, whom I hesitate to nominate for canonization under any ecclesiastical auspices. In his
lifetime he was more often the object of the dis-
approbation than the approval of churchly
groups, and his own anticlericalism was both the

cause and the result of religious opposition to
him. He had a rather low opinion of clergymen,
though not so low as he had of kings. The two
groups he regarded as being in varying degrees
tyrannical. Without straining the meaning of
words, however, one can say that in the advocacy
of education as well as of democracy the Sage
of Monticello was profoundly a man of faith.
However rationalistic he may have been when
he surveyed theology, he was little short of
emotional when he spoke of education; and until
this day he remains a fount of inspiration to all
who have answered his clarion call to a crusade
against ignorance. The words that he wrote to
DuPont de Nemours more than a century ago
(1816) will doubtless echo through all the ages
that democracy shall endure: "Enlighten the
people generally, and tyranny and oppressions of
body and mind will vanish like evil spirits at the
dawn of day."

In this age, when the shadow of tyranny hangs
over so much of the world, we would do well to
return to this quickening faith. Enlightenment
is not enough, but it is much; and, unquestionably, it is still sorely needed. Civic faith such as
Jefferson proclaimed and exemplified may lead
no soul into an ecclesiastical pathway of salvation,
but it has inspired countless men and women who
have labored for the common good, and it can

still inspire a bewildered democracy. The apostles of public education who have followed him have, almost without exception, hailed him as their chief.

Many of them have been described, and have described themselves, as reformers. They have seen evils to be combated and overcome, but in emphasis they have had to be positive. In the course of his famous controversy with the Boston schoolmasters, who set themselves up as defenders of the existing order, Horace Mann said: "On schools and teachers I rely more than on any other earthly instrumentality, for the prosperity and honor of the state, and for the reformation and advancement of the race. All other reforms seek to abolish specific ills; education is preventive."[1] Unlike the Abolitionists, the leaders of the educational reformation did not content themselves with attacking an institution which they regarded as sinful. They attacked the tyrant Ignorance, but since he can be overcome only by enlightenment, theirs was the task of providing opportunities. They were not primarily destroyers, as moral reformers so often are, but architects and builders.

The leaders whom we shall consider here, however, I am venturing to describe as evan-

[1] *Reply to the "Remarks" of Thirty-One Boston Schoolmasters* (1844), p. 3.

gelists. Most of them (not including Jefferson)
were noted as speakers and campaigners. It is
for this reason, in part, that they are better known
than quieter men and women who were concerned chiefly with daily teaching and the devel-
oping of institutions. As a group, these men
performed their most conspicuous service in
arousing public opinion by appeals not untinged
with emotion. It is appropriate, therefore, to
describe them as evangelists; and in the term itself may be perceived their characteristic strength
and weakness.

In the North the most notable of them appeared in the generation before the Civil War,
when public education could be appropriately
advocated as a corollary and safeguard of political democracy. As in the case of their contemporaries the Abolitionists, with whom they were
generally sympathetic, they came most frequently from New England, where the ferment
of reform was working, though the influences
which they set in motion became most effective
in the Middle West, as was also true with the
Abolitionists. By the time of the Civil War the
philosophy of universal public education, on the
elementary level at least, came to prevail in the
entire free-state area, though the crusade continued long afterward. In terms of actual

growth, the great period of public high schools did not begin until the turn of the century.

In the South comparable developments in the common schools did not come until later. Distinct progress in public education was made in certain states, notably in North Carolina, before the Civil War, but in general the aristocratic social system made democratic educational appeals relatively unpopular. The war itself prevented further developments, and no effective scheme of public education could be projected until after the horrors of Reconstruction were past. The Southern educational crusade continued, in one form or another, until the World War. The movement in the South was strikingly similar to the earlier one in the North, though it had a distinct local and regional flavor. The Southern educational crusaders, living close to the soil, had a pungency and heartiness that was rarely equaled in the colder clime, and perhaps they may be described as more characteristically evangelical.

The chief figure in the Northern revival was Horace Mann, and he served as a direct inspiration also to the Southern leaders. As an educational evangelist he richly deserves the primacy which tradition has accorded him, though some of his contemporaries doubtless made greater technical contributions to theory and practice.

His prominence in the crusade dates from his appointment to the newly created post of secretary to the Massachusetts Board of Education in 1837. A number of people, including many schoolmasters, thought that the appointment should have gone to James Gordon Carter, who was chairman of the committee that framed the bill and had had far greater practical experience than Mann and had done far more to attract attention to the needs of the public schools. If Carter had been named, he would very probably have gained a more prominent place in history instead of soon passing into relative obscurity. There is much that is fortuitous in fame, but it is doubtful if Carter, with all his unselfish devotion to the cause, or if anybody else, could have brought to this task the same fortunate combination of qualities and gifts that Mann did or could have exercised as conspicuous leadership.

Another leader who might have challenged Horace Mann's priority was Calvin Ellis Stowe, who is now more readily recognized as the husband of Harriet Beecher. There are disadvantages in having a famous wife. Calvin Stowe married her in Cincinnati, while he was a professor in Lane Theological Seminary, and he strove to improve public education in Cincinnati and the West before *Uncle Tom's Cabin* was written or Horace Mann had given up the practice of law.

In 1836 Stowe was sent to Europe by the State
of Ohio to investigate educational systems, and
he published in the following year a *Report on
Elementary Instruction in Europe* that was
widely distributed and very influential. Stowe,
however, was a clergyman, primarily interested
in Biblical scholarship. His activities were not
concentrated upon public education, so he was
overshadowed by Mann as he was by his wife.
A large man, with a great beard, he was a picturesque as well as a saintly figure, but he was not
and did not want to be dramatic, so others gained
a greater share of glory.

Somewhat later in time than Horace Mann,
and second only to him in recognized influence,
was Henry Barnard of Connecticut. His term
of office as commissioner of education, a similar
position to that of Mann in Massachusetts, was
cut short by legislative action, so he transferred
his labors for a time to Rhode Island, where, as
in his native commonwealth, he was a pioneer in
educational statesmanship. Most of his later
service, and perhaps his greatest service, was rendered through the *American Journal of Education,* which he edited for more than a quarter of
a century (1855-1882) and into which he put
his entire personal fortune. His contributions
were more technical than those of Mann and in
this respect were doubtless greater. Relying less

on the spoken word, he was less notable as an evangelist, and, in the narrow sense, he was less religious; at least, it is not known that he belonged to any church. However, he was a man of deep faith with a lifelong passion for public service. Unquestionably, he should be placed high on the roll of saints of education, and he would receive more extended notice here but for the fact that his colaborer in Massachusetts serves as a better symbol and example of the particular things I have in mind.

The story of Horace Mann's career is so well known that it need be told only in barest outline. He was born on a farm in Franklin, Massachusetts, toward the end of the eighteenth century, and grew up under conditions of considerable privation. Whether or not the inadequacies of his early education were overemphasized by him in after years for dramatic contrast, he was late in going to college. At Brown, however, his record was brilliant and won him first honors in his class. His oration at graduation was on the subject, "Progressive Character of the Human Race," which was always his favorite theme.[2] For more than a dozen years he was a practising lawyer, first at Dedham, Massachusetts, and then, after the tragic death of his young wife, in Boston. In view of his abilities and his rule

---

[2] Comment of his wife in *Life and Works* (1891), Vol. I, p. 28.

that he would take no client in whose cause he did not believe, it is not surprising that he won the vast majority of his cases. He gained prominence in political as well as legal circles, serving in the legislature for a decade. He was president of the State Senate in 1837 when the famous bill was passed, creating a board of education, and was asked to serve as its secretary.

Much to the surprise of everybody except those who knew him best, he accepted. His salary was set at $1,500 which, in his estimation, would allow him $500 for ordinary expenses after the extraordinary expenses of the office, including extensive travel, had been met. He was a childless widower and did not want much. In his journal he wrote these words: "Well, one thing is certain: if I live, and have health, I will be revenged on them; I will do more than $1,500 worth of good."[3] According to his second wife, Mary Peabody, sister-in-law of Hawthorne, whom he married in mid-career, his health and his animal spirits were always feeble, though he worked as a rule eighteen hours a day. Certainly he did good that was beyond financial estimation. As he predicted, posterity became his client.

For approximately a dozen years, until 1848, when he was elected as an antislavery Whig to succeed John Quincy Adams in the federal

[3] April 18, 1838, *Life and Works*, Vol. I, p. 102.

House of Representatives, he was secretary of the Board of Education, touring the state, holding conventions and teachers' institutes, establishing the first American normal schools, encouraging libraries, editing a school journal, issuing annual reports that were read throughout the United States and even in other nations. In 1852 he was the unsuccessful candidate of the Free-Soilers for the governorship of Massachusetts, and that year he became president of the new Antioch College in Ohio, where he remained until his death in 1859. The concluding words of his last baccalaureate address, which was also his last public speech, have become immortal: "Be ashamed to die until you have won some victory for humanity."

His political service was but a minor episode, and his dramatic and tragic presidency of a struggling Midwestern college was but an epilogue to his main career. His entrance into the field of public education had been somewhat accidental, but through his originally obscure office in Massachusetts he found the all-absorbing mission his temperament required. Until this day he is spoken of as the father of the common schools not only of his state but the nation.

It is not as an educational statesman that we shall describe him here, but as a lay saint and evangelist. It is important, therefore, to say

something of his religion.   This passionate humanitarian had scant sympathy for the rigid
Calvinism in which he was born and bred.   In
later life he declared that the joy of his youth
was blighted by "theological inculcations."   For
half a century the church in Franklin was ruled
by the Rev. Dr. Nathanael Emmons, whom
Mann afterward described as a "hyper-Calvinist
—a man of pure intellect, whose logic was never
softened in its severity by the infusion of any
kindliness of sentiment."[4]   He even seized upon
the occasion of the funeral of Horace's brother to
preach a sermon on "dying unconverted."   At a
later time Mann himself may have been hyper-
critical in speaking of his old pastor, but he made
it perfectly clear in innumerable references in his
Journal that he would have nothing to do with
the sort of God that Doctor Emmons proclaimed.
In mature life he was a Unitarian, on terms of
friendship with William Ellery Channing and
Theodore Parker.

Most of the attacks on him and the Board of
Education with respect to the alleged irreligion
of the public schools, he attributed to the old-line
Calvinists, whom he often referred to in private
as the "Orthodox."   More than any other religious group they had a vested interest in the
maintenance of the old order.   Speaking of an

---

[4] *Life and Works*, Vol. I, p. 13.

attack of this sort, he said in his *Journal:* "Probably they will have no difficulty in making out that the Board is irreligious; for with them religion is synonymous with Calvin's five points. As for St. James's definition of it, 'Pure religion and undefiled is to visit the fatherless and widows in their affliction,' &c.; and that other definition, 'Do justly, love mercy, and walk humbly with thy God,'—the Orthodox have quite outgrown these obsolete notions, and have got a religion which can at once gratify their self-esteem and destructiveness. They shall not unclinch me from my labors for mankind."[5] Another year he wrote a friend: "The orthodox have hunted me this winter as though they were bloodhounds, and I a poor rabbit."[6] His annoyance with them was so great that, in private at least, he often called them bigots. Allowing himself to be drawn too far into controversy, he sometimes called names even in public.

Apart from personal resentment, he objected to these conservative churchmen because he was quite convinced that what they really wanted in the schools, if they could possibly restore it, was sectarianism of their own particular brand, while he knew that in schools which must serve an entire commonwealth, containing various sects, this

---

[5] *Life and Works,* Vol. I, p. 107.
[6] December 1, 1844, *Ibid.,* Vol. I, p. 230.

was no more practicable than desirable. He himself was definitely nonsectarian. When he went to Antioch College, he connected himself with the Disciples of Christ, under whose auspices the institution was conducted, because he thought this action would help him to influence the students in the right direction. He was the more willing because in theory this religious group was strongly opposed to sectarianism. It is also clear that in religious and theological matters he was a liberal, as in educational matters he was a progressive.

Mann said upon several occasions that he was in favor of conservative reform, that is, of pulling down something bad when he had something good with which to replace it. So far as religion was concerned, the bad thing was narrowness and intolerance; the good thing was broad human sympathy. No one who reads the entries in his *Journal* or his comments on religion in the schools in his last annual report, could ever accuse him of lack of spirituality or of negativeness in his emphasis. Speaking of the Massachusetts system of public schools, with which he was now severing his official connection, he said:

"In a social and political sense, it is a *free* school system. It knows no distinction of rich and poor, of bond or free, or between those, who, in the imperfect light of this world, are seeking, through different avenues, to reach the gate of heaven. Without money and without price, it throws open its doors, and spreads the table of its bounty, for all the children of the state. Like the sun, it shines not only upon the good, but upon the evil, that they may become good; and, like the rain, its blessings descend not only upon the just, but upon the unjust, that their injustice may depart from them, and be known no more."[7] Here is not merely a report, but a sermon; and here is evangelical fervor. Yet, with all his revolt against the rigidities of his native Calvinism, Mann was never able to free himself fully from its spell. The successive tasks that came to him he assumed almost as a fatalist. And in his doctrine there was more than a shadow of theology. All children were born, not in sin it may be, but in ignorance, and they must be saved from damnation through education.[8] He never would have denied that he was a preacher of salvation.

If it be true, as has been said, that Mann was a Puritan without a theology, he was in morals unquestionably a Puritan of an austere and rigid sort. He admitted that he had always been exempt from the common vices: intoxication, profanity, and, most of all, tobacco. In this last

[7] *Life and Works,* Vol. IV, p. 336.
[8] See Paul Bixler, "Horace Mann—Mustard Seed," *American Scholar,* Vol. VII (1938), p. 25, for a stimulating comment on this.

respect he went beyond his old pastor, who was a
chewer of the "vile weed." The report and reso-
lutions which he drafted for an association of
Ohio teachers in 1856 on the subject of tobacco
revealed two at least of the fundamental weak-
nesses of this extraordinarily humane man: his
lack of humor, despite his wit; and his tendency
to train heavy artillery on very small game.[9] His
liberalism did not extend to personal morals: he
wanted his purity to be simon pure.

His brother-in-law, Nathaniel Hawthorne,
appears not to have liked him very much. He
did not fully approve of Hawthorne either, and
administered a moral rebuke to him when he first
detected him smoking a cigar. Also, Mann had
a low opinion of novels, even though Hawthorne
wrote them. As a man with a mission, the crusading Secretary of the Board of Education did
not intend to be enslaved by any habit or to be
distracted by mere entertainment. He liked contact with intelligent minds, but was impatient
with those whose lives were not purposeful. His
wife emphasized his love of children, but her
nephew, Julian Hawthorne, doubted if he ever
understood them.[10] Whether he did or not, he
was determined that they should have their
chance.

[9] *Life and Works,* Vol. I, pp. 574-79.
[10] Bixler, p. 25.

The characteristic which allies him most closely with the religious enthusiasts, the saints and martyrs of the ages, was his utter absorption in a cause. As so often happens even with the greatest men, he sometimes identified methods and personal opinions about which wise and good men may well disagree, with general purposes, which many of his opponents may have held in common with him. Attacks on methods and opinions need not be regarded as attacks on a cause itself. But if he identified his cause with himself, certainly he submerged himself in it. Again and again he speaks of "the cause," "our cause," "the good cause," "the great work," "the momentous work," "the revival." He exulted in its progress, and was profoundly depressed by all manifestations of indifference toward it. He often refers to "preaching a preachment," and he may properly be described as an evangelist of light. Toward those who, in his opinion, were blind to the light or sinned against it, he could be pitiless; but the measure of his indignation was the measure of his consecration.

An important test of the character of anyone is his devotion to his purposes; but we esteem no man as great unless he seems, also, to have shown intelligence in the choice of purposes. By both of these standards, Horace Mann attains impressive stature. It may be hyperbolic to say, as he did, that the common school is the greatest of human discoveries, but unquestionably the common school is one of the supreme manifestations of the democratic faith.   Public education as practiced has proved no panacea for human ills, but no one can deny the glory of the conception. Even in the incomplete and imperfect form that we have known it, it is one of the finest examples that history affords of preventive social medicine. This dauntless crusader identified himself with a cause greater than sect or party.   Specific means and instrumentalities may change, but the struggle for general enlightenment will go on as long as hope survives in the human breast.   So there is far-seeing statesmanship as well as evangelical fervor in Horace Mann's ringing words.

In his last report he said: "We are part of a mighty nation, which has just embarked upon the grandest experiment ever yet attempted upon earth,—the experiment of the capacity of mankind for the wise and righteous government of themselves.   Fearful are the issues which hang upon the trial, but few and simple the conditions that predestine the result.   The firmament, though pillared upon rottenness, shall be upheld, and the light of day shall continue to revisit the earth, though the sun be blotted out, sooner than a republic shall stand which has not knowledge and virtue for its foundations. . . . Yet, in more

than one-half of these States, no provision
worthy of the name is made for replenishing the
common mind with knowledge, or of training the
common heart to virtue. . . . The sower who
would scatter the elements of knowledge and virtue amongst them must press forward with
gigantic strides, and cast his seed with a gigantic
arm."[11]

The seeds sowed by Horace Mann fell into
many minds; and many men, perceiving the
sweep of his arm, were inspirited to emulate his
example. Before proceeding to the Southern
harvest field, I should like to pay passing tribute
to one of his later followers in Massachusetts,
whose service of half a century to the cause of
public education ended only a few years ago. He
may serve as an example of latter-day evangelists
of the New England school. Albert Edward
Winship, born in Massachusetts, taught for a
time in public and normal schools, became a Congregational minister, and was appointed in 1883
a secretary of a commission of his church that
was active in educational work in the West. In
1886 he resigned this post to become editor of
the *Journal of Education*, published in Boston.
He continued in this work for forty-seven years,
and also edited for a time the *American Teacher*,
besides writing a number of books. Through these

[11] *Life and Works*, Vol. IV, p. 337.

means, and also by lectures in all parts of the
United States, he spread the gospel of free and
democratic schools, and won for himself the title,
"the circuit rider of American education."

The Southern evangelists of education can
stand on their own record, but no one would be
quicker than they to acknowledge their indebt-
edness to the Northern movement and to Horace
Mann. The connection between the two crusades is exemplified in an episode in the life of
J. L. M. Curry, who was born in Georgia and
graduated from the University of that state, but
who also studied law at Harvard in the 1840's.
There, incidentally, he had as a classmate Rutherford B. Hayes. While in Cambridge, Curry
heard William Lloyd Garrison and Wendell
Phillips speak, but was cold to the pleadings of
what he described as a "noisy and fanatical fac-
tion." Indeed, he remained until the Civil War,
he said, an adherent of the Calhoun school of
politics.

However, he gained an unforgettable impression of Horace Mann. Aghast at the destructive
spirit of the Abolitionists, he was completely
captivated by the constructiveness of the Secretary of the Board of Education. "When I was in
Cambridge," said Curry, "there occurred the
celebrated controversy, since historic, between
Horace Mann and the thirty-one Boston teach-

ers. Mann's glowing periods, earnest enthusiasm, and democratic ideas fired my young mind and heart; and since that time I have been an enthusiastic and consistent advocate of universal education."[12] Not until after the War did Curry turn from politics and law to the major activity of his life, but the seeds that fell in his fertile mind sprouted much earlier. As a state legislator in antebellum Alabama, he says that he always voted for measures in favor of education.[13]

These diverse geographical references may be confusing, so it would be well to tell briefly the story of a career that is not as generally known as it ought to be.

Jabez Lamar Monroe Curry, who sometimes expressed impatience at the superabundance of his names, was born in Lincoln County, Georgia, in the angle formed by the Savannah and Little Rivers and long known as "The Dark Corner" because of the lawlessness which prevailed there. His father was a farmer, who owned slaves, and a country merchant. The boy attended an "oldfield" school and went for a time, across the river in South Carolina, to the famous school then conducted by the sons of Moses Waddel, teacher of

[12] E. A. Alderman and A. C. Gordon, *J. L. M. Curry: A Biography* (1911), p. 75.
[13] *Ibid.*, p. 95.

Calhoun.   While he was in his early teens, the
family moved to Alabama, where his father engaged in similar activities as in Georgia, besides
being postmaster.

Curry went back to his native state to attend
the University of Georgia, which he afterward
described as a solid, old-fashioned institution,
and a very pleasant one in which to live. Curry
stood high in his class and was already noted as a
speaker. After studying law at Harvard under
Joseph Story and Simon Greenleaf, he returned
to Alabama, where he engaged in agriculture,
politics, and law, as the ablest Southerners of his
generation were prone to do. He served for several years in the state legislature and was for two
terms in the federal Congress, leaving that body
with the outbreak of war. He was a member of
the Confederate Congress and, later, a lieuten-
ant-colonel in the Confederate Army. For his
years his record was excellent, but it was in the
prevailing pattern. In the dark days after Appo-
mattox he turned to religion and education as
the chief mainstay and hope of a discouraged
people.

In his early life Curry's parents were not pro-
fessing Christians, but were distinctly moral
people and regular attendants on such church
services as there were. Only Methodist and
Baptist preachers visited "The Dark Corner" in

Lincoln County, Georgia. At least one colored Baptist preacher came there and was heard gladly by whites as well as blacks. Curry's people were Baptists by inclination and, in Alabama about the time of the Mexican War, his father was baptized, after a "protracted" meeting. The son soon followed. He was always moral, he said, but had no religious convictions in his youth and had no "rapturous experiences" even now. Until the war he was an active layman, very hospitable to visiting preachers, as his father had always been.

After the war he turned to religion "as the one eternal thing to which a man of soul could repair amid the overthrow of all old standards."[14] In the summer of 1865 he preached a regular sermon; in the fall he was elected president of Howard College, a small Baptist institution, as General Lee was elected president of little Washington College in Virginia; and in January, 1866, he was ordained as a Baptist minister. Throughout the rest of his eventful life he did a good deal of preaching, and he liked it; he was invited to many regular pastorates, but never thought it his duty to become "exclusively a preacher."

After three years as president of Howard College he became a professor in Richmond College

[14] Alderman and Gordon, p. 194.

(now University of Richmond), where he remained more than a dozen years. He had now begun to collect honorary degrees, so he could be called either "Colonel" or "Doctor." During this time he was offered a post in the Cabinet by his old friend, President Rutherford B. Hayes. In 1881, on nomination of General Grant, he was elected agent of the Peabody Fund (created in 1866) for the advancement of education in the South, in succession to Barnas Sears, a New Englander. From this time the educational movement in the region came increasingly into the hands of natives, though it continued for long years to be strongly supported by Northern interest and philanthropy. Except for an interval of three years, when Curry served as American minister to Spain, under Cleveland, he remained in this post until his death, and in 1890 he also became agent of the George F. Slater Fund for the education of Negroes in the South. In 1899 he was president of the conference on education in the South, from which developed the Southern Education Board. Through these and other contacts Curry was associated with practically all the leaders in the Southern educational revival and inspired them with his zeal.

Into the details of the multifarious activities of this zealous, eloquent, and warmhearted man, we need not enter here. As a former congressman and Confederate officer he was a welcome speaker before state legislatures and other audiences whom he sought to educate to a new sense of public responsibility. Through the operation of the funds which he represented he was a powerful influence in the establishment of normal schools and systems of graded schools, and in his body of reports and speeches he created a large body of educational literature. The ideas that he expressed were not new: Horace Mann had said much the same thing a generation earlier. But he adapted them to the elemental needs of his own people and served, more than any Southerner of his generation, to create a public opinion favorable to these causes. In a special sense he belongs to the whole Southern people. Born in Georgia, he was buried in Hollywood Cemetery, Richmond, where the dust of Jefferson Davis lies, and in due course he was chosen as one of the two representatives of Alabama in Statuary Hall in the Capitol in Washington.

In Curry and those who came after him one does not perceive the same certainty of divine approval that has so generally characterized the reformers and crusaders who have come from New England. Not as in the Abolitionists, or even in Horace Mann, was there the unshakable conviction of the absolute righteousness of their cause and of the black iniquity of the opposition.

Among a people who had suffered so grievously ignorance was properly regarded, not as sin, but as misfortune; and opposition must be met, not by fiery denunciation, but by persuasive argument. Financial generosity had to be cultivated among a people who had little to give. In Curry's time, at least, there was less need to chide the Southern people for social selfishness than to inspire in them a new faith in a trained democracy. "The education, and proper training of the voters" he regarded as "a sacred duty which cannot be neglected without injury to the State and to society. Ignorance is no remedy for anything."[15] The opposition of individualists and denominationalists was met by emphasis on the immensity of the task. "Without State system and support," said Curry, "general education is impossible. Parental and individual and church efforts have never approximated the needs of the young."[16]

As a Baptist, Curry was in theory a Calvinist, but his theology had none of the grimness of New England. As a minister of the gospel who had once been a high public official, he saw no conflict between Church and State. His hope lay in their co-operation. In Louisville he said, in 1883: "What of the night? I can only answer:

[15] Alderman and Gordon, p. 413.
[16] *Ibid.*

Do what lies nearest in the light of duty and conscience and the Scriptures, and leave results to God. If any safe solution there is, it must be in the school-house and church house, in education, and in the gospel of Jesus Christ. . . . Education . . . does not cure social and political ills. It must be supplemented by and allied to the uplifting, renovating, regenerating power of the Christian religion."[17] To the sophisticated his words may appear as truisms, but I prefer to perceive in them, not theological doctrine, but stirring expressions of faith in an age when men believed in education as they believed in God. Curry was a bearer of good tidings.

Not all of the Southern educational leaders who followed Curry were as religious as he was, or enjoyed such harmonious relations with the churches. Indeed, many of them, especially those who were concerned chiefly with public education at the college and university level, met with considerable clerical opposition in behalf of denominational institutions. But he can be regarded as the symbol of a movement in which many men participated. The outstanding leaders, like Charles D. McIver and Edwin A. Alderman of North Carolina, were, almost without exception, bred in churches in which the evangelical spirit was strong. In spirit and even in

[17] Alderman and Gordon, p. 412.

methods they reflected the evangelism into which
they had been born and with which they were
thoroughly familiar. They themselves described
their "message" as the "gospel" of popular education; the institutes and popular conventions that
they held were, despite the emphasis on instruction, not unlike "protracted meetings"; their
informal gatherings among themselves were, in
effect, testimony meetings, designed to renew
their consecration; they toured states like so
many revivalists; they proclaimed the needs of
children with the enthusiasm and emotional fervor hitherto associated with sermons about personal salvation. Some of them were notable
builders of institutions, but it is not unfair to say
that they were most successful as quickeners of
public interest and creators of public enthusiasm.
Both in their strength and in their limitations
they were evangelists.

It does not seem desirable to describe the careers of any of them in detail, but, rather, to
speak of two other men, one a governor of a
Southern commonwealth, who more than any
public man of his generation translated enthusiasm for education into political action, and the
other the greatest educational leader yet produced by the Negro race. We shall speak, all
too inadequately, of Governor Charles B.
Aycock, who represents North Carolina in Statu-

ary Hall in the Capitol at Washington, as Curry does Alabama; and of Booker T. Washington.

Charles B. Aycock, governor of North Carolina during the first quadrennium of the present century, said that he was inspired to his educational mission by seeing his mother make her mark because she was unable to sign her name. In 1912, toward the end of the era marked by the outbreak of the World War, he made the last speech of his life in Birmingham, Alabama, where he was introduced by the Governor of the state as the Southern governor who had done most for education. He reported with pride that since his inauguration as governor a schoolhouse had been built in North Carolina every day, including Sundays. I want to give you a few extracts from the speech he made on the subject of universal education. It not only illustrates the passionate enthusiasm of a Southern educational crusader; it also presents this "cause" in elemental and appealingly human form. Here the stump speaker or revivalist, speaking for common men, uses language which they can perfectly understand.

"... I believe in universal education; I believe in educating everybody. I will go further, and say that I believe in educating everything; and so do you when you come to think about it.

"What do you mean by education? You mean

bringing out of a thing what God Almighty put into it. . . . Why, we have educated the Irish potato. You know what an Irish potato is now; but what did the Irish potato used to be when it was ignorant and had never gone to school? . . .

"So education is good for a vegetable, and it is good for animals, and it is good for a mule. You know the most dangerous thing in this country is an old, unbroken mule. . . .

"Well, if it is good for a mule, it is good for a dog. . . . Yes, it is good for dogs. Well, if it is, it is good for human beings. That is, to bring out of them all that there is in them. You understand, if there is not anything in them, you can't get anything out of them. But the question I put to you is, Who appointed you to say that there isn't anything in this little child? . . . No, God hasn't conferred that power upon any of us; but He has said to us all, 'Open wide the schoolhouses and give to every child the opportunity to develop all there is in him.' If God didn't put anything there, you and I can't bring it out; but if you and I suffer the light of such a one to be hidden under a bushel, may the sin and shame of it abide on us forevermore. . . .

" . . . You cannot talk to an audience that cannot hear. Governor, did you ever try it? Well, I have. When I was governor I made speeches all over North Carolina. I canvassed the state for four years in behalf of education of the children of the state, right straight along; sometimes on Sundays they would ask me down to the churches to talk, and I always talked about education."[18]

At this point he fell dead.

One notable aspect of the educational crusade in the South in the generation which ended with the World War was the friendliness which was manifested by its leaders toward the education of the Negroes. Faced as they were by the problem of elevating standards among the whites in a region that had been devastated by war and paralyzed by social revolution, they naturally gave first emphasis to the crying needs of their own race; but no one more than they sought to remove extreme race prejudice from the Southern mind and to gain for the Negroes a modicum of educational opportunity. The man with whom they most gladly co-operated was Booker T. Washington, greatest of American Negroes. No list of saints and statesmen of American education would be complete without his name.

In one sense it is inappropriate to describe him as an evangelist of education. Admirable as were his powers of speech, his chief contribution to his own people, and to the whites as well, was his

---

[18] R. D. W. Connor and Clarence Poe, *The Life and Speeches of Charles Brantley Aycock* (1912), pp. 316-24.

demonstration of the effectiveness, the dignity, and the beauty of honest human labor. The trappings of learning he did not despise, but his most famous injunction was "Cast down your buckets where you are." This might well serve as a motto elsewhere than in schools for the training of Negroes in mechanical tasks.

My father heard the principal of Tuskegee Institute make his famous speech at the Atlanta Exposition in 1893, and some years later, as a youth in Georgia, I gained a firsthand impression of the fruits of his instruction. A colored carpenter, who was a graduate of Tuskegee, was doing some work in my father's office and I was spending a good deal of time watching him. At a fairly advanced stage in the operations, it became evident that instructions had been unwisely given and that some of the construction must be taken down and begun anew. The carpenter was unhappy about the mistake, though it was really no fault of his. To me he said, "No workman likes to think that anything he does is so badly done that it must be done over again." Thus did a little Southern boy learn from a colored carpenter an unforgettable lesson in the pride of honest craftsmanship. With such a lesson, any form of education may properly begin.

The story of Booker T. Washington is too well known to require retelling, but we can at least place him here in the goodly company of apostles of education. That he gained inspiration, as he did his English style, from daily study of the Bible is a matter of common knowledge. He must often have read in the thirteenth chapter of the First Epistle to the Corinthians about the Christian charity which he proclaimed and practiced. Even more than his words, his works spoke for him.

In conclusion, may I say just one word about the significance for our own times of the spirit of such men as these, Northern and Southern, white and black. During the cynical decades which followed the World War, there was much merriment in sophisticated circles at the expense of advocates and practitioners of public education. In our own sobered and discouraged era there is more inclination to review the optimistic prophecies of earlier days, and to inquire how far they have failed of fulfillment. To what extent the high hopes of the educational evangelists have been and have not been realized is a matter of opinion. It seems clear, however, that the failures of civilization in the last quarter of a century, of which we are now so painfully aware, cannot be attributed primarily to the inadequacies of the gospel of universal education, any more than to the insufficiencies of the gospel of Christianity.

Chiefly they have been due to war and depression, to political and economic impotence in the face of unexampled complications.

Educators have erred in permitting themselves to be lost in the mazes of methodology, just as clergymen in times past have wandered foolishly in the barren abstractions of theology. But perplexing as are the problems which teachers face in the efforts to adjust their pupils to the vast complexities of modern life, they need not be apostates to their historic faith, which was so profoundly Christian. Indeed, it has never been more important than now to return to elemental truths and fundamental doctrines, and to renew faith in universal education, adapted to individual needs and capacities, as the first requirement of an enduring democracy. On it the persistence of both Church and State depends.

VI

SECULAR SAINTS OF LEARNING

IT will be admitted without dispute that the
prevailing trend of higher education in
America since the Civil War has been in the direction of secularization. Everybody knows that
our oldest privately endowed institutions were of
religious origin and that many of them remained
for generations under close clerical supervision.
Denominational institutions of high rank remain,
with varying degrees of sectarian control, but it
will be generally agreed that, except in Catholic
institutions, the ecclesiastical tie has been weak-
ened everywhere, even when it has not been
severed. Meanwhile, state institutions have been
established on a secular basis and in recent decades
these have grown greatly in strength and influence.

Only a few of the reasons for this trend need
even be mentioned here. To a considerable degree they have been practical reasons, though no
one can claim that we have followed a reasoned
plan of institutional development, designed to
avoid unnecessary duplication of function. Also,
though the growing religious tolerance which
marked the generation that ended with the

World War may be attributed in part to indifference, it was due in considerable part to an increasing recognition of the similarities rather than the dissimilarities of religious groups. The intelligent men of the era may not have been fully aware of that fact, but in their thoughts of religion and education they were moving from the particular toward the general. Among scholars themselves this trend was so strong that it became overwhelming. As they conceived it, scholarship was essentially universal in its spirit. The fearful attempts that have been made in Europe in our own time to set it up on a nationalistic or racial basis have made all of us the more aware of the universality of scholarship as understood in all the countries of the civilized world in better days.

As seekers for universal truth, without regard to nation, race, or creed, scholars have sought the largest possible freedom from the control of particularistic groups, as, indeed, they have sought freedom from external control of every sort. Professors don't like political dominance any better than denominational, and almost everywhere now their greatest fear is that minds may be fettered by the power of the State. In this country, however, the tradition of governmental power has been relatively weak, and circumstances have permitted scholars to gain large independence of the organized Church.

It will naturally be asked if one is likely to find many saints in the increasingly secularized institutions of higher learning of the last half-century. At certain times a majority of regular church-goers might have responded in the negative. To many of them a college or university that was presided over by a layman seemed a godless place. Occasional clergymen are still to be found among high educational executives, but even in church schools laymen are likely to be in control. One finds scientists in seats once occupied by ministers alone and professors who are under no compulsion to go to church. If the Spirit of God moves in them, it does not move in the old-fashioned way.

In the generations between the Civil War and the turn of the century there were many notable college and university presidents who were not only churchly but ministerial. With the accession of Charles W. Eliot in 1869 the clerical tradition was broken at Harvard, thus confirming the suspicions which many godly people already had of that ancient seat of learning. During Eliot's day, however, Yale was directed by three successive Congregational ministers, Theodore Dwight Woolsey, Noah Porter, and the second Timothy Dwight. In Cambridge this was doubtless regarded as further proof of the backwardness of Yale. Dear old Noah Porter, as a matter

of fact, opposed most of the major tendencies in
education which were destined to prevail. However, the clerical line was broken with the election of Arthur Twining Hadley, an eminent
economist, in 1899. Princeton had two Presbyterian theologians in succession: the redoubtable
James McCosh, who surprised many of his breth-
ren, however, by accepting the doctrine of evolution; and Francis L. Patton, whom Woodrow
Wilson succeeded in 1902. Meanwhile, E.
Benjamin Andrews, a Baptist minister, served at
Brown; and subsequently he presided over the
University of Nebraska. In New England the
ministerial tradition lingered longer in the colleges; many will remember Hyde of Bowdoin.
During the first generation of our own century
there were clerical presidents in some institutions
that were not closely connected with particular
churches. After serving at Smith College,
Marion LeRoy Burton, an eloquent Congregational minister, was president successively of the
Universities of Minnesota and Michigan. Other
illustrations could be cited, but they would not
disprove the assertion that there was everywhere
increasing lay emphasis and secular control.

Among such men as these one could easily find
notable examples of saintly scholars, as one could
among individual professors in almost any institution. It is no reflection upon them that we

shall concentrate here upon another type. The men whom we shall consider furthered rather than opposed secularization as a necessary step in the progress of science and learning. Almost without exception they were definitely spiritual and regular communicants of churches, but they also found in scholarship itself a sort of religion, as Horace Mann found one in the cause of public education, and as Jane Addams did in her settlement work. Many of them would deny that they were saints, but nearly all of them would admit that they were secular.

The comment is the more pertinent because these men, as a rule, grew up in just the sort of homes that might have been expected to produce ministers. It has been my personal observation, though I am not in position to support it with statistics, that the scholarly group in America in the last generation, as well as in the one before it, was recruited to a marked degree from what we might call the old religious stock. This has not been true to the same extent, I suppose, since the World War; and at all times some of the recruits of learning have come from queer groups and odd places. In all the faculties with which I have personally been familiar, however, a strong religious background could have been safely assumed. In almost all of them there have been many sons or at least grandsons of ministers. Indeed, the manse, the rectory, and the parsonage have been richly represented in every important phase of American achievement.

Almost anybody can cite specific examples of ministers' sons from academic rosters. From my own memory I will mention a few just to set other minds to working: Woodrow Wilson and his successor as president of Princeton, John Grier Hibben; two presidents of the University of Chicago, Ernest DeWitt Burton (who was himself ordained) and Robert M. Hutchins; George E. Vincent, formerly dean at Chicago and president of the University of Minnesota; President Benjamin Ide Wheeler of the University of Chicago; Chancellor James H. Kirkland of Vanderbilt; Dean LeBaron R. Briggs of Harvard.

From rolls of professors the list could be almost indefinitely expanded. In some men I know and in others I suspect that the religious impulse was deflected into scholarship. Where their fathers talked of seeking God they spoke of seeking truth; and to a greater or less degree they proclaimed the doctrine of salvation by learning. In the first flush of its enthusiasm at least, modern scholarship in America was based on an almost religious faith in the power of truth and enlightenment. Abundant evidence can be found in the careers of the most noted university presidents of the generation which ended, roughly, with the World War.

To evangelicals or ritualists there may have appeared to be little that could properly be termed religious in the spirit of the best-known educational leader of the generation after the Civil War, Charles W. Eliot. By good Methodists and good Catholics alike he was sometimes referred to, doubtless, as an unbeliever. As has been said, he dissented "from most of the creeds of the dominant churches of Christendom, and of some of them he did not hesitate to speak with reprobation, or even with abhorrence. As a consequence, his nonconformity was frequently interpreted as heresy, and his faith as unbelief."[1]

As a Unitarian, however, Eliot was distinctly churchly. His father, though never ordained, studied divinity; he was for long years warden and choirmaster of King's Chapel, Boston, and trained his children in a rational, undogmatic faith. Charles W. Eliot married the daughter of the minister of that church, but she died the month that he was elected president of Harvard, leaving the care of two small boys to a widower of thirty-five. Every Sunday evening he had these boys repeat to him selections of religious poetry, and on cruises in the summer he awakened them

---

[1] F. G. Peabody, *Reminiscences of Present-Day Saints* (Boston and New York, Houghton Mifflin Co., 1927), p. 299.

with a morning hymn. One of them became a
minister. Eliot himself, throughout his long
life, was a regular attendant and communicant of
the church, and he frequently spoke at Unitarian
gatherings. No one who reads any of those
speeches that have been preserved can deny that
this austere man had a serene religious faith. In
this faith men who knew him best saw the secret
of his confidence and courage.

Francis G. Peabody, who knew him for seventy years, included a chapter on him in his book,
Reminiscences of Present-Day Saints, but was
sure that he would have vigorously protested.
To him the word "saint" implied selfrighteous-
ness; he thought that no one could be a real
saint if he were conscious of it. An heir of the
stern Puritan tradition who had been schooled to
the ways of science, he was not one to bare his
soul to the onlooker. But to his lifelong friend
this bold educational leader who trampled rough-
shod on opposition was completely selfless.
"President Eliot's courage," he said, "was not
self-display, but self-effacement; not the audac-
ity of vanity, but the fearlessness of faith."[2] As
Unitarianism represents Protestantism in perhaps
its most rational form, so Eliot, though essentially a man of action, represents religious intellectualism at almost its purest and best. As per-

_____
[2] *Reminiscences of Present-Day Saints*, p. 301.

sonified in him it may be too self-confident and severe to be endearing or to be typical of a whole generation of scholars, but it commands profound respect.

Three decades ago he delivered at a summer school of theology a lecture on "The Religion of the Future,"[3] in which he predicted the disappearance of religions of authority, of anthropomorphism, of asceticism. There would be, he said, a new idea of God, comprehending "the Jewish Jehovah, the Christian Universal Father, the modern physicist's omnipresent and exhaustless Energy, and the biological conception of Vital Force."[4] The thought of God would thus be consistent with the revelations of science and also with "all the tenderest and loveliest teachings which have come to us out of the past."

To his bold mind it appeared that this future religion would not only be "in harmony with the great secular movements of modern society— democracy, individualism, social idealism, the zest for education, the spirit of research, the modern tendency to welcome the new, the fresh powers of preventive medicine, and the recent advances in business and industrial ethics—but also in essential agreement with the direct, personal

---

[3] Eliot, *The Durable Satisfactions of Life* (1910), pp. 157-97.
[4] *Ibid.*, p. 169.

teachings of Jesus, as they are reported in the Gospels."[5]

After the World War broke out he realized that his counsels of perfection would not immediately prevail, but he saw in the insufficiency of the churches in that crisis but another demonstration that Christianity had been paralyzed by authoritarianism and obscured by dogma and had, as a matter of fact, never been really tried.[6]

The religious faith of this man whose mind was so luminous and so bold was, of course, inseparable from his unshakable belief in education, in the ultimate triumph of intelligence, and in the power of the human mind itself. Into this pattern many of his major policies as an educator can be fitted—the elective system, the use of the case system in the teaching of law, even the abolition of compulsion in attendance upon chapel. All these and many other policies revealed his optimistic belief in the trustworthiness of the human mind when left unfettered. In the figure and the words of Eliot, then, there is an extraordinary symbolism. Here in stark simplicity appears the faith of a generation of intellectuals, a faith which waxed with the successive triumphs of science, which confidently envisaged

[5] *The Durable Satisfactions of Life*, p. 197.
[6] "The Crying Need of a Renewed Christianity," December 29, 1914, in *A Late Harvest* (Boston, Atlantic Monthly Press, 1924), pp. 213-44.

the solution of social problems and the further triumphs of democracy, and which was thought to be in essential harmony with the fundamental teachings of Jesus after the trappings of ritualism and dogmatism had been torn away.

It was revealed in 1914 and has become even more apparent in the quarter of a century since that neither original Christianity nor the liberated intelligence of humanity has triumphed. Clearly the great liberals, from Thomas Jefferson to Charles W. Eliot, were too optimistic in their judgment of human nature and minimized the destructive as well as the elevating power of emotion. Of the philosophical limitations of Harvard's most famous president others can speak better than I; but to students of human personality this luminous and fearless rationalist seems magnificent but rather cold. One must warm the heart at some other fire. Nonetheless, in our age of passion, hysteria, and obfuscation, there in the frozen North is a star of calm reason to which the eye can turn.

Many have found a corrective to sheer intellectualism in the warm philosophy of William James, who had been trained to science in Eliot's Harvard, but who also had inherited from his Swedenborgian father a certain predisposition to religious mysticism. Although I began these lectures with a reference to this great thinker,

and have been influenced during all my mature
life by his emphasis upon experience and faith,
I am neither disposed nor qualified to enter into
the profundities of philosophy. I cannot even
use the terms correctly. So I must confine myself to men of action and their everyday beliefs.
The emphasis here is upon university presidents
during a period when so many of them were
great.

To the general public, Daniel Coit Gilman,
first president of The Johns Hopkins University, is not so well known as Eliot; but in academic circles it is generally agreed that no single
institution was more responsible for the development of American scholarship and the advancement of medical education in the last quarter of
the nineteenth century than the one which he
directed during that period. Established by what
was then regarded as a princely bequest, Johns
Hopkins was not destined to have such a share of
subsequent munificence as the oldest institutions
in the East or the University of Chicago, but in
the training of the scholars of a creative era it was
excelled by none, if, indeed, it was equaled. The
later part of Eliot's work at Harvard and the
brilliant achievements of Harper at Chicago
might have been impossible without it.

Daniel Coit Gilman was born in a Connecticut
town, went to New York City with his family in

his fourteenth year, and then went in due course to Yale. Afterward he spent a couple of immensely fruitful years abroad with his collegemate and lifelong friend, Andrew D. White, first president of Cornell. Those were times in which educational pioneers were bred. From his father Gilman appears to have inherited his temperament and to have inherited or acquired his altruistic spirit. He grew up in the Congregational Church and while at Yale he was one of a group of students who established a Sunday school for poor children in a backward section of New Haven. At all times he disliked cant and casual talk about religion but, as he wrote a friend, he regarded the "giving of oneself" as the most important thing in Christianity and in life.

During his trip abroad he wrote his sister that he was still uncertain what he should do, but that he looked "more and more to the ministry" as the place where he could probably do the most good.[7] However, he said that he would have to talk about everyday things and the application of Christianity to common life. What he wanted to do was to act upon the minds of men for the elevation and improvement of society. While he was in Saint Petersburg in 1854 as an attaché of the American Legation, he was asked to conduct services in the American Chapel after the

[7] Fabian Franklin, *The Life of Daniel Coit Gilman* (1910), p. 28.

departure of the regular pastor, but because of his own impending departure for Berlin, if for no other reason, he declined the invitation. It may be noted in passing that he had an elder brother who was a Congregational minister. After Gilman's return to the United States, when he had a post in the Yale Library, he sought and obtained a license to preach in order that he might accept occasional invitations. Probably he never accepted many of them, but it was in the same spirit of helpfulness to humanity that he entered into the pursuit of science.

For seventeen years he was at Yale, in the library, as professor of geography, and as a moving force in the Sheffield Scientific School. He might have been president of the University of Wisconsin or first president of the University of California. He did accept a renewed offer from the latter institution, and in California he might have remained, despite sore vexations from an interfering legislature, had not the opportunity to create a new sort of institution in Baltimore been afforded him. Here trustees and president were to be free to work out their own ideas of human betterment without the menace of meddling politicians. A university and a hospital were to be established. In one note that he made he speaks of the expected millions as having been "consecrated" to these objects. In the centennial year of the United States this experiment was begun by a scientist who had a profound desire to be useful.

The historical events need not be recounted here, though the continuous and conspicuously successful efforts of the president to enlist great scholars and personalities rather than to erect impressive buildings deserve the fullest commemoration. One likes to pay all the tribute he can to a faculty which contained on its roster such names as Basil L. Gildersleeve, Dr. William H. Welch, and Dr. William Osler. Our concern here, however, is with the personality of the creator and the spirit of his creation.

The nonsectarianism of the university aroused much criticism at the beginning, though the president and the trustees were notably religious men, and, as it happened, the first small faculty of six was drawn mostly from ministerial families. To some minds it seemed that the false god of science was being worshiped. At least there was violent criticism of the opening of the university with a lecture by Huxley, without a prayer. One irate clergyman wrote: "It was bad enough to invite Huxley. It were better to have asked God to be present. It would have been absurd to ask them both."[8]

To Gilman the God of science and the Uni-

---

[8] Gilman, *The Launching of a University* (1906), pp. 22-23.

versal Father of Humanity were one, but his own later comments on this early outcry were couched in his customary language of temperance and common sense: "I wish it were possible," he said, "for religious people to agree upon what should be taught to the young, in respect to religious doctrine, or at least to unite in religious worship, yet I cannot forget that, in ages and countries where one authority has been recognized and obeyed, neither intellect nor morals have attained their highest development."[9]

That there was in the new institution a spirit to which the exaltations of religion itself may be compared is the testimony of those who were present during its springtime. One of the best comments came fifteen years later from Josiah Royce, whose spirituality is not likely to be questioned. "The beginning of the Johns Hopkins University was a dawn wherein 'twas bliss to be alive.' Freedom and wise counsel were enjoyed together. . . . One longed to be a doer of the word, and not a hearer only, a creator of his own infinitesimal fraction of a product, bound in God's name to produce it when the time came."[10]

In this environment were trained an extraordinary number of the pioneers of American scholarship during what was perhaps its most

[9] *The Launching of a University*, p. 24.
[10] Franklin, p. 229.

fruitful generation. The list is much too long
to be given, so, besides Royce, I will merely mention a quartet of historians, gladly hailed within
their guild as masters: Frederick J. Turner and
Charles H. Haskins, J. Franklin Jameson and
Charles M. Andrews—not to speak of Woodrow
Wilson or one of Gildersleeve's pupils, Walter
Hines Page. Apart from their great personal
achievements, these men have seemed to me most
notable for their spirit. They went forth as crusaders in the cause of truth, more assured than
their disciples have been able to be that they
could find it and that it would prevail.

At the center of the whole group of scholars
was Gilman, more reticent than even in his youth,
but with an extraordinary ability to detect latent
talent and to discover men to themselves. For a
quarter of a century he remained there, weather-
ing unexpected storms, then for a few years he
directed the Carnegie Institution in Washington,
and in 1908 he died. The "fresh courage of life"
did not forsake him and, without losing sight of
his clear-purposed goal, he remained patient
despite obstacles and delay. His wife said that
the secret was partly temperamental, but that a
deeper root was his "unshakable faith in God's
providence." To her he would often say, when
prospects were clouded, "The Lord Reigns";

and in this conviction he renewed his strength.[11]
It might be said of him as it was of Eliot that
his was a selfless life.

Scholars themselves are now aware of the
limitations of the modified German methods of
investigation and teaching which he and his colleagues did so much to introduce, but they will
always be grateful for the beneficent zeal of
these pioneers. It is doubtless as great a mistake
to lose oneself in learning as in the transports of
religious mysticism, but no one can question
that the opening of the avenues of the mind to
the treasures of science and history was an incal-
culable benefit to American society and to mankind.

From Gilman one naturally proceeds to Andrew D. White, who graduated from Yale the
next year after him and went with him to Europe,
and who also became the creator of a great university. White was a historian, not a scientist, and
besides launching Cornell he had a distinguished
career as a diplomatist. As a pathmaking teacher
of history at the University of Michigan, he cut
across the boundaries of nations, and as the first
president of the new institution at Ithaca he de-
barred all distinctions of sex, race, or creed.
There was a universality of spirit in these creators,
and none of them more than White believed

[11] Franklin, p. 429.

wholeheartedly in the universals of humanity, of science, of religion, of truth.

Like Eliot and Gilman, he was secular in believing that learning should be entirely free from ecclesiastical control; and his book, *The History of the Warfare of Science and Theology in Christendom*, published after he left Cornell, may have made him the least popular of the three with theologians. But there can be no question of his deep reverence and genuine religious faith. He was born in New York state of New England stock, but his parents had revolted from Calvinism and become Episcopalians. Throughout life he was a loyal member of his church, serving from time to time as vestryman. In his *Autobiography* he has left a full account of the development of his religious ideas, putting it in the last chapters, doubtless, because of his recognition of the importance of the subject. Far more than his friend Gilman, he studied the variety of forms in which the religious spirit has manifested itself in history; and, despite all the things he said about theologians, he did not go as far as Eliot in insistence on rationality. Probably it would have been difficult for one bred to the rich and stately ritual of the Episcopal Church to be entirely at home in the cold, clear light of Unitarianism. As a student of history he recognized that a degree of imperfection and inade-

quacy is to be expected in forms of belief or cere-
monial, though there is no reason to suppose that
he went as far as certain modern physicists who
have perceived an unexpected fuzziness in nature
itself. He did not expect men to breathe pure
ether, and said that we take our oxygen diluted
with other gases. Yet, with the optimism which
characterized his generation, he believed that religion was evolving into higher and purer forms.
As he was in his young manhood a strong advocate of antislavery and in his later years an advocate of peace, in the middle years of educational
statesmanship he was, like his great colleagues, an
unfailing and optimistic advocate of unfettered
learning and investigation. He urged upon students that they adopt causes; and the major cause
in which his rich mind was enlisted was that of
freedom, which in his opinion provided the necessary atmosphere for human progress.

The torch of learning, like that of religion, is
passed from hand to hand. So we may properly
turn, if only for a moment, to one of Andrew D.
White's pupils at Michigan, whom he inspired to
historical work and who succeeded him as president of Cornell, and who went seven years later
to his field of greatest service as president of the
University of Wisconsin. Charles Kendall
Adams did not go to college until after he was
grown, and had to work his way when he did

go. He was born in Vermont and brought up there and in Iowa, mostly on the farm. He was not as brilliant as the man whose historical work he carried on at Michigan, but he is credited with having introduced the seminar method of teaching there. There was a look about his eyes which caused him to be given the nickname "Droopy," though as a student he was known as "Dig." When he was at Cornell, before his second wife forced him to trim his straggling beard, he was known as "Farmer Adams," but in the end he became a distinctly impressive figure, both looking and acting like a president.

Upon three universities he left the mark of a strong and kindly personality. Always he was pious and the most faithful of Congregationalists. To the country folk he undoubtedly seemed a Christian of the good, old-fashioned sort. One incident, related by his friend Benjamin Ide Wheeler, later president of the University of California, will help to place him in the gallery of devotees of learning. In Adams's first year at Cornell, Wheeler first met him and gained no impression of brilliancy. The new President seemed heavy, bucolic, uncouth. In the evening they walked over the campus, still undeveloped, raw, and gloomy. "This might be a great university," said Wheeler, "but a man just from Harvard would have to be excused for not seeing

it. He saw it, though. We came to the brow
of the hill that overlooks the lights of the valley
and commands the dim expanse of the lake to the
north, and there he stopped and struck his cane
on the ground. 'Here the great library will
stand,' he said. His voice had a new ring. The
drag and lethargy were gone. The enthusiasm of
faith and creative foresight had come to the front;
the chill had departed, swallowed up in a great
heart interest, and departed forever, for so far as
I was concerned I never noted it again, so long as
I knew him."[12] Much the same sort of thrill
might have been felt by the builder of a trans-
continental railroad. There were some striking
similarities between the men who opened up the
West and the men who built universities, but
there was in these great academics a rarer faith, a
faith in books and the treasures they contain. At
Madison, Wisconsin, again Adams built a library.
"At last we have done something worthy of the
state," he said. To this great and selfless builder
the library undoubtedly stood as a supreme symbol of faith in intelligence itself.

A library was erected as a special memorial
to William Rainey Harper, first president and
creator of the University of Chicago, who was
perhaps the least secular and probably the most

[12] C. F. Smith, *Charles Kendall Adams* (University of Wisconsin, Madison, 1924), p. 32.

vigorous of all these saints. In connection with him one must think of books, but one also thinks of dynamos. A railroad president once told him that he ought to have *his* job; and in energy and power of personality he may be compared not inappropriately with Commodore Vanderbilt, James J. Hill, or any of the magnates of transportation or industry in his expansive age. Yet this extraordinary genius who has been described as three giants in one since he was notable as a scholar, a teacher, and an administrator, first gained fame as an instructor in Hebrew.

There was a fortuitous element in his embracing this very ancient language, though the youth who took a Doctor's degree before he was nineteen, after writing a dissertation in which the prepositions in Latin, Greek, Sanskrit, and Gothic were compared, must have had a knack for languages. It just happened that there was somebody to teach a small class in Hebrew in the little college at which Harper graduated at the age of fourteen. This incredibly dynamic personality impresses the observer as one who created or transformed environment, rather than as one who was determined by it, but he was impressionable as well as creative and under other circumstances might have directed his course into other channels. He might have been president of a railroad, or President of the United States, but, as fortune would have it, he became the greatest teacher of the Old Testament that this country has ever produced, and one of the most conspicuous advocates during his generation of the extension of all manner of learning to the public at large.

To the story of a career which has become a legend we cannot hope to add any important facts, but a brief outline is necessary for any comprehension or orientation of the man. His life began in the village of New Concord in Muskingum County, Ohio, and his parents were of the stock of Scotch Covenanters. The community consisted of United Presbyterians; a "psalm-singing community" it has been called. The boy knew the Scriptures before he knew much else. He played croquet and marbles, learned to skate, and in due course became the leading member of the village band, but he delighted in reading and study even more than in music. He graduated at Muskingum College at an amazingly early age, and while clerking thereafter in his father's store kept up his study of languages and even taught them in the college. Then he went to Yale and to his triumph over the ancient prepositions.

Perhaps, in these years, his passion for linguistic learning was greater than his zeal for righteousness. At any rate, he did not become offi-

cially a church member until he was teaching
Latin and Greek in the preparatory school of
Denison University, and by this chance circum-
stance he became identified with the Baptists.
His religion appears never to have bordered on
the mystical or the speculative. It was of the
forthright sort, like that of Amos and other
prophetic figures whom he was destined to resur-
rect.

His zeal for Hebrew, not for theology, brought
him as a teacher to the Baptist Union Theological
Seminary at Morgan Park (Chicago), where
during his first year he did enough studying on
the side to acquire a degree in divinity. Ere
long a group of students, whose volition was
spurred by his tempestuous enthusiasm, spent a
Christmas vacation reading the Hebrew Old
Testament eight hours a day; and the young instructor had established a summer school of Hebrew and was teaching the beloved language by
mail. Before he left Morgan Park at the age
of thirty to accept a professorship at Yale, thirty
summer schools had sprung up under his inspiration and his correspondence pupils numbered a
thousand. Meanwhile, he had tossed off three
or four books and started several scholarly
magazines.

During five years at Yale he was fed by this
same unquenchable fire and had as astounding

results. The following meager description gives
an idea of his activities during his last year: "He
was at the same time professor of Semitic languages in Yale University, instructor in Hebrew
in Yale Divinity School, and Woolsey Professor
of Biblical Literature in Yale College; he was
president of the American Publication Society of
Hebrew; principal of the American Institute of
Sacred Literature, through which he conducted
his Correspondence Schools; principal of the
Chautauqua College of Liberal Arts; editor of
two journals, then known as the *Old and New
Testament Student* and *Hebraica*; and conducted
four lecture courses outside of Yale—in Brook-
lyn, Vassar, Boston, and New Haven."[13]

Our history affords no parallel to this demonic
promotion of sacred studies. To attain the salvation he so lustily proclaimed men had to follow
the hard road of learning; in the Hebrew Scriptures they were to find truth and see God. In
Harper the spirit of the pioneer, the promoter,
and the prophet were conjoined. In his quest
there was no place for idleness or weakness. He
told one of his classes at Chautauqua: "You are
neither to eat, drink, nor sleep. You will recite
three times a day, six days a week. Study nothing
but Hebrew. Go to no side interest. Begin with

[13] T. W. Goodspeed, *William Rainey Harper* (University of Chicago
Press, 1928), p. 96.

the rising of the sun Monday and stop with the chimes Saturday night."[14] Yet they did not hate him; they adored him.

It is no wonder they wanted him to inaugurate the new University of Chicago, but he was unwilling to undertake it unless there was reasonable hope that the plan he had formulated for "the Great University" could be carried out. A mere college did not interest him. The auspices were to be Baptist and, until recently, the president had to be of that church, but in practice Harper couldn't be anything but interdenominational. The story of his achievements at Chicago need not be told. The luxuriance of his educational imagination was immediately manifest. It stunned even the wealth and munificence of Rockefeller and, superb as the achievement was, it fell short of his ideal. Not that he really hoped to teach everybody Hebrew, but through research and teaching of the first order in all fields, through scholarly periodicals which he founded in profusion, through the pioneer University Press which he created, through summer sessions and correspondence courses, he sought to gain for learning a domain like that of Alexander. Though he became, perforce, an American pioneer of higher criticism, his religious faith remained unclouded and his personal piety continued to be

[14] Goodspeed, p. 69.

simple and utterly sincere. He can best be described, perhaps, as an evangelist who proclaimed and to an extraordinary degree·effected salvation by learning. He pressed on, tirelessly, heroically, toward goals which would have seemed unattainable to anybody else. Only death could quench the fire that burned within him. If Charles W. Eliot was the North Star of higher learning in his generation, Harper was its Southern Cross.

These exemplars of free learning and builders of universities may be regarded as pioneers and creators in an expansive age. The educators and scholars whose careers have fallen in the postwar era can hardly hope to equal the greatest of them in tangible achievement. To men who have lived through war and depression and have witnessed the exile of learning from lands where once it flowered the scholars of the prewar generation seem fortunate in the age in which they lived. They are most to be envied for their buoyant faith. Despite all the obstacles they faced, they had little thought of failure. They were confident that the beneficent empire of the mind would be continually extended until it embraced all mankind.

Most of the clouds which now hang over academic groves have drifted in from without, but even had there been no world-wide spiritual depression scholars would have found it difficult to recapture the first fine, careless rapture of pioneering days. Even in normal times they might have been expected to settle down to more humdrum tasks and to perform them in a more pedestrian spirit. In the development of a university no less than in the development of a church, men tend to become involved in mechanics and technique, to overemphasize means and lose sight of ends; and in the case of scholarship no less than religion, faith needs to be perpetually renewed. The secularism of learning need never be feared so long as the beneficence of its purposes is clearly perceived; and selfish pedantry is unlikely when the heart is warmed with inner fires. It may be that the spiritual challenge of our times will serve, both in church and school, to clarify our minds, purify our hearts, and steel our wills. Great men we may never be, but we shall have abundant opportunity to battle for the God of humanity and of truth.

If historic circumstances made it natural in the past in our country for the religious impulse to express itself in action, the present situation in the world at large seems to be a peculiarly difficult one for saints. Out of anarchy, tribal chiefs have emerged and before them their subjects quail. Before the days of Hitler and Mussolini,

William James wrote: "Compared with these beaked and taloned graspers of the world, saints are herbivorous animals, tame and harmless barnyard poultry."[15] To an age that glorifies pagan force, saints may be ill adapted, but, as James also said, they are adapted to that higher society of which prophets have spoken and poets sung and the hope of which men will surrender only with life itself.   That they will continue to appear in America and other lands we cannot doubt; and that their strength will come from the spiritual emotions that surge within them we can be sure.

---

[15] *The Varieties of Religious Experience*, p. 372.

INDEX

Abolitionists, 63-83; compared with suffragists, 101-02
Adams, Charles Kendall, 168-70
Adams, John Quincy, 15, 77, 124
Addams, Jane, 108-13, 153; comments on saints, 7-8
Alderman, Edwin A., 141
Andrews, E. Benjamin, 152
Anglican-Episcopalians, 35, 36
Anthony, Susan B., 89, 96, 98-100, 102
Appletons' Cyclopaedia of American Biography, 32
Asbury, Francis, 44, 52, 53
Aycock, Charles B., 143-45

Backus, Isaac, 46, 51, 53
Bacon, Leonard, 40
Baptists, 36, 46, 48
Barnard, Henry, 122-23
Barton, Clara, 107-08
Beecher, Catherine, 92
Beecher, Henry Ward, 39, 51, 54, 75, 91
Beecher, Lyman, 74, 92
Birney, James G., 72, 75
Blaine, James G., 16
Bloomer, Amelia Jenks, 103
British Isles, birthplace of eminent American clergymen, 52
Brooks, Phillips, 42-43, 50, 54, 55
Brown, John, 64-66
Bryan, William Jennings, 15-16
Burton, Marion LeRoy, 152
Bushnell, Horace, 39, 50, 54

Calhoun, John C., 15-16
Campbell, Alexander, 46, 52, 54
Carroll, John, 46, 54
Catholics, Roman, 35, 36, 44-46, 48

Channing, William Ellery, 41, 54, 108, 126
Clay, Henry, 15
Clemens, Samuel L. (Mark Twain), 18
Clergymen, 28, 32ff.; chronological distribution of, 53ff.; college and university presidents, 151-52; sons among noted educators, 154
Comstock, Anthony, 61-62
Congregationalists, 35, 39-41, 47-51
Cotton, John, 40
Curry, Jabez Lamar Monroe, 134-41

Dana, Charles A., 26
Davenport, John, 40
Denominations, distribution of distinguished clergymen among, 37ff.
Dictionary of American Biography, 32, 33, 85
Disciples of Christ, 46
Dix, Dorothea L., 26, 108
Dwight, Timothy (1752-1817), 40, 50, 54
Dwight, Timothy (1828-1916), 151

Eddy, Mary Baker, 51, 84
Education, higher: secular trend since Civil War, 149-52; saints, 152ff.
Education, public: crusaders for, 114ff.; in North and South, 119-20; characteristics of Southern leaders, 139-40; significance of spirit of crusaders, 147-48
Educators, women, 105ff.

INDEX

INDEX